Understanding Man

Understanding Man

How We Got to Where We Are

RAY C. STEDMAN

MULTNOMAH · PRESS

Portland, Oregon 97266

Unless otherwise indicated, all Scripture quotations are from the Revised Standard Version of the Bible, copyright 1946, 1952, © 1971, 1973, Division of Christian Education, National Council of the Churches of Christ in the USA.

Cover design by Phil Malyon and Judy Quinn
Cover photo by Steve Terrill

UNDERSTANDING MAN
© 1975 by Ray C. Stedman
Published by Multnomah Press
Portland, Oregon 97266

Published in cooperation with Discovery Foundation, Palo Alto, California.

Printed in the United States of America

Library of Congress Cataloging-in-Publication Data

Stedman, Ray C.
  Understanding man.

  Reprint. Originally published: Waco: Word Books, c 1975.
    1. Man (Christian theology) I. Title.
BT701.2.S74   1986   233   86- 16463
ISBN 0-88070-156-0 (pbk.)

86 87 88 89 90 91 – 10 9 8 7 6 5 4 3 2 1

CONTENTS

PREFACE

In this brief study on *Understanding Man*, I have attempted to bring into focus some of the principles of true psychology and true anthropology. It is by these biblical principles that all secular studies concerning mankind must be measured, for here is a revelation of things as they really are.

Our task is to find clues to unravel the greatest mystery ever written—the story of man. We are seeking to understand ourselves, both as men and women "in Adam" and also as the new men and women we have become if we are "in Christ." But we must begin with the first Adam because what he was, we are.

It always strikes me as strange that anyone can deny the reality of the story of the Fall of man, especially when the very person who denies it is himself repeating it, perhaps dozens of times a day. Temptation follows the same pattern with us that it did with Eve in the garden of Eden, and the process is relentless.

Sometimes we may think our guilt is hidden from God's eyes, since no one else knows about it and no judgment has befallen us. Yet within us, whenever we yield to evil, a darkness falls and death tightens its grip upon our throat.

Here, then, is a study aimed first at understanding the unchanging process of temptation, and then at grasping the unchanging process of God's grace which seeks us out and restores us.

But the grace of God often goes unrecognized for what it is. In this passage of Genesis, God has revealed clearly how unwilling he is that any should perish. Far from merely pronouncing judgment on Adam and Eve, he gives them an assurance of life beyond the death of their bodies, and a sure promise of a Redeemer to come.

I hope your heart will be lifted with fresh encouragement as you discover the loving purpose behind God's expulsion of the first man and woman from the garden. On that purpose hangs the whole truth of the gospel of Christ.

Ray C. Stedman

1
WAS ADAM
FOR REAL?

In the early stages of writing this book, I sat in the airport of Guatemala City, facing a large mural depicting life among the ancient Maya Indians. Under the shadow of great volcanoes which had rumbled and muttered all afternoon, I thought of the history of the Mayas—that strange race we know so little about—and I felt anew the mystery of history. Civilizations have risen and flourished for centuries, then suddenly, often for unknown reasons, have died and are now buried in humid jungles, forgotten fragments of ancient history.

The question came to me again as it comes to any who think about the past: Where did our human race begin? How did these strange beings come into existence? For what purpose?

These questions have forever fascinated us. To my knowledge only one book answers them reliably. Scientists, of course, are trying to discover facts from the ancient past, though even they admit their efforts are but a kind of groping in the dark for a few fragments. Yet this book of God, bearing upon it the seal and authority of the Lord Jesus Christ, has revealed to us everything we need to know to solve life's riddle. Here is all we need to know about humanity—revealed in Scripture, especially designed that we might know the facts about life.

It is no exaggeration to say there are no writings more important for the proper understanding of history and man than the first chapters of Genesis. Here is uncovered the secret of man's sinfulness, that terrible mystery of evil and darkness which continually confronts us. In this section is the key to the relationship of the sexes and the proper view of marriage, plus the solutions to the mounting divorce rates and other marital issues abounding in modern society.

This section explains our struggles to survive, throwing great light on the issues of work and leisure. In these chapters is the first and fundamental revelation of divine redemption and grace, and here the essential groundwork is laid for understanding the cross of Jesus Christ.

These chapters are unparalleled in importance. But because they are so important, they have been heavily attacked, and rejected outright as repugnant to modern man. Certain cults treat them as utterly inconsistent with what man should believe about himself.

Sometimes these passages have been contemptuously dismissed as a mere collection of ancient myths or legends with no significance for modern minds. Others treat them as containing important truths, but needing to be (in the favorite word of many in theological circles) "demythologized." To quote one of the writers of this school:

> *There is truth of great vitality and power in many passages of which the strictly historical accuracy may be questioned. It is our job therefore to find the truth that may be buried under some layers of legend.*

Before I discuss the meaning and intense significance of these passages, I must first dispose of these objections. Many are bothered by these problems, and lest we seem to ignore them, I want to deal with them now, before we come to the actual meaning of the passage.

The Documentary Theory

There are two general lines of attack on the story of Adam and Eve in the garden of Eden. One tries to destroy the literary integrity of the text; the other denies its historical accuracy.

The first approach claims that this section of Genesis (and probably everything from Genesis through Deuteronomy) was written not by Moses, as the Bible indicates, but by an unknown editor (whom these scholars call a redactor) who lived long after David and Solomon, and who may have lived even as late as the Babylonian captivity, only some five centuries before Christ.

These critics claim that the redactor was not writing down things revealed to him by any divine process, but only recording tales he had heard, like those told by women gathered around wells and discussing various legends from the past, or by travelers with strange stories from far-off places. These critics say he collected these tales and others, and thus recorded for posterity these early legends.

Support for this idea arises out of certain changes of style in this passage and the use of the divine name in a different form. In Genesis 2:4, for example, the name translated in English as "the LORD God" appears for the first time. In Genesis 1 there is only the name *God,* which is a translation of the Hebrew *Elohim.* But here we have *the LORD God*, or in Hebrew, *Yahweh Elohim*, and all through this section that name is used. It was therefore suggested that various stories and changes in authorship could be detected by the use of the divine names.

This evolved into what is called "the documentary theory" of the authorship of Genesis: Some unknown editor collected from various sources these documents, which can be identified by certain marks, and combined them into a single unit. Using excerpts from here and there, the editor blended them into the books we now know as Genesis, Exodus, Leviticus, Numbers, and Deuteronomy—the Pentateuch, the five books of Moses.

This idea has been supported by certain piecemeal evidence taken from the Scriptures. Scholars have gone through the books and extracted certain passages that seemed to support their theory, while ignoring others that would contradict it. This documentary theory gained wide support, but long ago was fully answered by both Jewish and Christian scholars. Remarkably, however, it still persists, though it is increasingly difficult to defend.

Fifty years ago Dr. Lyman Abbott spoke at the University of California at Berkeley. He was at that time a noted liberal scholar working on the origin of scriptural books. He said something like this: "Young

gentlemen, I feel that perhaps I am as qualified as anyone to speak in this field of the origins of the books of
the Bible, and I want to warn you against going too
far in basing your conclusions upon the so-called 'assured results of modern scholarship.' As one of these
modern scholars, I know that these results are not always as 'assured' as they seem to be. My careful conclusion is that the first five books of the Bible were
written either by Moses—or by someone else named
Moses!" Perhaps this is as far as we need to go in laying to rest the documentary theory of the Scriptures.

No Talking Serpent

The second attack upon this section is more frequently pressed today. This is the idea that there are
great truths about man here—his fears, his evil, his
hungers, all set forth in a remarkable way that teaches
us much about ourselves—but that these truths are
conveyed deliberately in the language of myth. Moses
may have written this, they say, or perhaps some unknown writer or writers did. But at any rate, the text
is an attempt to convey mighty truths through the
language of myth, adopting a kind of parable in order
to convey these truths. There was no literal tree in a
literal garden; there were no actual beings named
Adam and Eve; and of course, there was no talking
serpent or forbidden fruit.

It is all somewhat like the myth of Santa Claus.
Everyone today (except Virginia) knows there is no
real Santa Claus; but the ideas behind Santa Claus—
cheerful jollity, a reward for good behavior, and a universal kindness of spirit—are all true. If we forget the
myth of Santa Claus we still have a core of truth conveyed to us by the story of Santa Claus. We can treat
these opening chapters of Genesis in much the same
way. You can take the story of Adam and Eve, they

say, throw away the form by which it is conveyed, and still have a germ of truth about the human race.

But have you? What do we say to this kind of approach? We must reject it as biblically untenable, scientifically unsound, and in the end totally destructive of truth and faith. Let me explain why.

First, this approach violates the integrity of Genesis. Where does myth end and history begin? Where is the line of demarcation? If Adam and Eve are a myth, then so is the story of Cain and Abel. And if Cain and Abel are a myth, then so are Noah and the flood. Since the record moves right on without a break into the stories of Abraham, Isaac, and Jacob, are we to assume that these, too, are myths? If so, where does history begin? How can you detect where myth, fantasy, and legend end, and actual human history begins?

Such a process carries right over into the New Testament. The story of Christ's virgin birth becomes a myth, as does even the story of his incarnation itself. The Christmas story becomes nothing but a beautiful parable, designed to express truth, but not true in history. The same interpretation goes with the stories of the miracles of Jesus and his resurrection and his ascension. Where do you stop?

The answer is that you cannot stop, once you begin. There is no stopping place when you apply this kind of theory to the biblical records! Of course, if you treat the Bible that way, you must in all good conscience treat any other ancient document in the same way. If you carry this out to its logical conclusion, we are left without any trustworthy knowledge of the ancient world. Obviously, this view of Scripture destroys too much to be acceptable.

Yet if we honestly examine the first chapter of Genesis, we can see that it is not a myth at all. It accords with the discoveries of modern science, and in fact, anticipates and corrects much of modern science.

Furthermore, passages throughout both testaments warn against believing in myths or taking them seriously. The apostles were aware of this kind of danger to faith and warned against it even in the early days of Christianity. Paul writes to Timothy, his son in the faith, and warns him against being influenced by godless myths and old wives' fables (1 Timothy 4:7). Peter stresses that the accounts given by him and the other apostles were not cleverly designed myths, but were actual historic occurrences (2 Peter 1:16).

There are parables and legends reported to us in the Bible. You can find them in both the Old and New Testaments. But the significant thing is that the writers of Scripture were aware of their nature and clearly presented them for what they are.

Beginning with Moses

Second, the mythic view of Genesis contradicts the teaching of the Lord Jesus Christ and of the apostles.

If you believe the story of Adam and Eve is a myth, you immediately clash with the authority of the Lord Jesus Christ. Matthew records that our Lord answered the questions of the Pharisees about divorce with the statement, "He who made them from the beginning made them male and female" (Matthew 19:4). If you accept this as a statement from One who declared himself to be the truth and who told only the truth, then you must accept this story of Adam and Eve as factual.

The Lord Jesus constantly referred to Moses as the author of the Pentateuch. Again and again he said that what Moses wrote, he himself fulfilled. In the wonderful scene in Luke after his resurrection, where he walked unrecognized with two men along the Emmaus road, he asked them why they were so downcast and sorrowful. They told him of the strange events in Jerusalem, how one Jesus of Nazareth was crucified. And then we read, "Beginning with Moses and all the prophets, he interpreted to them in all the Scriptures the things concerning himself" (Luke 24:27). Later he appeared to the disciples and rebuked them because they had not believed Moses and the prophets in the things written about him.

Never once did our Lord suggest that the historicity of anything in the Old Testament was to be questioned. He speaks of miracles—a source of many problems for critics today—in such a way as to confirm that they were historical events, including the account of Jonah inside the fish and other stories.

The apostle Paul also clearly viewed the early chapters of Genesis as fact. In both Romans and 1 Corinthians he compares Adam and Jesus, calling them both men, the heads of two separate races. In Romans 5:12-19 he speaks of Adam as the "one man" through whom sin and death entered the world, and of "the one man Jesus Christ" as the one through whom redemption came. If Jesus was a historical person, then Adam was too. In 1 Corinthians 15:21-22 and 15:45 Paul again views the two as individuals and compares them, pointing out that we suffer death through Adam, but that in Christ we are born again to new life.

In Paul's second letter to the Corinthians, he speaks of his fear that as the serpent deceived Eve, so the thoughts of his readers would be led astray by Satan's cunning (2 Corinthians 11:3). In 1 Timothy 2:13-14, Paul reminded Timothy that Adam was made first, and then Eve, just as the story in Genesis tells us. He says further that Adam was not deceived, but Eve was, and thus Adam went into sin deliberately, but Eve was blinded.

Therefore, if we view the accounts in the early chapters of Genesis as myths and legends and not real, historical events, we proclaim that the apostle Paul knew less than we know about such matters.

Third, the whole idea of myth ultimately destroys the teaching of Scripture and biblical theology. Why do men invent these suggestions of myth? If you investigate their reasons (though they may seldom admit this) it is often because they want to square these stories of Adam and Eve with the teachings of evolution. They do not want to admit there was a couple named Adam and Eve who began the human race; they would much rather teach that a group of hominids ascended from the animal kingdom and became men. The theory of evolution denies that humanity can be traced back to a single couple.

But if theories of human evolution are true, then there never was a fall of man. Either man was created perfect—in body, soul, and spirit, as Genesis tells us—or he has been slowly developing from the animal kingdom, and was never perfect. It is either one or the other. Either man fell from perfection or he was never perfect. If we believe man has never been perfect, certain fundamental questions immediately arise: What is the point of redemption? If we are simply moving toward an ultimate goal of perfection, then what was the value of Christ's work on the cross? Do we really need salvation? Are we not moving steadily toward a goal that will ultimately be reached, whether Christ died or not?

The moment mythical ideas are interjected into

the opening chapters of Genesis, there is an immediate clash with the doctrines of atonement and
man's redemption.

Demolished Claims

Finally, this mythical interpretation denies the scientific evidence which supports the historical truths
of these events. It has been almost humorous to see
how often in the last forty or fifty years the pompous
claims of the "higher critics" have been demolished
by the archaeologist's spade. Again and again evidence has turned up to prove that what the Bible says
is true and what the critics claim has been false. There
has not been one instance of the reverse, in which a
biblical event has been proved to be false by archaeology—not one!—but scores of instances where the
Bible has been substantiated.

There is, for instance, considerable archaeological
evidence that Nimrod, who is mentioned in the
fourth chapter of Genesis, existed as a historical person. Other characters in Genesis 4 whose historical
existence is supported by archaeology include
Lamech, his wife Zillah, and their son Tubal-Cain.
Their names have been preserved in ancient language
describing some of the activities in which they were
engaged.

Also in Genesis 4 is a statement that Cain, the son
of Adam, went out and built a city, naming it after
his son Enoch. Interestingly enough, ancient
cuneiform writings refer to a city named *Unuk*, which
is clearly related to this name *Enoch*—and it is called
simply "the city." This name *Enoch* later passed into
ancient languages as the word for city.

It is not unscientific to believe that Adam and Eve
and Cain and Abel were actual, individual human beings. There is nothing unscientific about their

stories, and no scientific evidence in any way gainsays them. Any claim of this sort is simply an attack upon this record to try to destroy confidence in these accounts, and thus to undermine the great and central teaching of the Scriptures concerning the redemption of man.

When we are done analyzing this, we stand where Christians have always stood, face to face with a choice: whether to accept the subjectivity of human wisdom or the authority of the Son of God. It is one or the other. Was Jesus right, or were the critics right? It is either Christ or the critics. It has always been and always will be.

I do not think there is any reason to debate the matter. I believe the Lord Jesus Christ stands as the final authority in every realm in which he speaks. When we consider the extent and nature of his authority and of his knowledge of the world and of the human race and the mind of man, and contrast these with the puny, finite knowledge of struggling, sinful, human beings who see through a glass darkly and who understand little of what they see, I find no real comparison.

This is why we must take these passages literally and treat them as historical accounts given to us to open our understanding to the problems we face daily. When we do, we discover they lavish upon us great and marvelous truths that help us understand life and rise in victory over the problems that beset us and the forces that oppose us.

May I therefore urge you, in reading these passages, to do as the Lord Jesus reminded us: Be like a little child who carefully, quietly listens to what he is told, thoughtfully reflecting on these things and not questioning whether they are right or wrong, historical or unhistorical. No one's mind is capable of establishing the authenticity of these passages today, and there is no evidence capable of disproving it. If we settle this, we can come to these accounts with minds open to the teaching of the Holy Spirit, remembering that as we come to know the truth about ourselves and our world, that truth will increasingly set us free.

2
THE MAKING OF MAN

Genesis 2 shows an obvious change of atmosphere from the chapter it follows. Genesis 1 was a simple narrative of the world's creation: the heaven and the earth, the plants and animals, and finally man. It is simple, yet majestic in its beauty and depth. Chapter 2 recapitulates—though in much greater detail—the main event of chapter 1: the creation of man.

Here also we find ideas introduced for the first time in the Bible. For instance, the name of God appears in a different form here. For the first time we have the great name of God that appears in so much of the rest of the Bible—*Yahweh Elohim*, translated in our versions as "LORD God." There is a special reason for this change. Chapter 1 deals with the making of things, and God is presented under the name of *Elohim*, the Creator. But when man appears on the scene, God is referred to by the name *Yahweh*, which essentially means the covenant-making God, the God who keeps a promise. This is particularly significant: When God first reveals himself to our race, it is as the God who intends to keep his promises.

Chapter 2 contains fascinating references to several fields of human thought. But the supreme aim of the chapter is unquestionably theological. The writer wants to bring us to the tree of the knowledge of good and evil in the garden of Eden, and thus to the testing of man, one of the most important revelations we have about our fallen race. But let us begin with a chronological note:

> *These are the generations of the heavens and the earth when they were created. In the day that the* LORD *God made the earth and the heavens, when no plant of the field was yet in the earth and no herb of the field had yet sprung up—for the Lord God had not caused it to rain upon the earth, and there was no man to till the ground; but a mist went up from the earth and watered the whole face of the ground—*then *the Lord God formed man (Genesis 2:4-7, emphasis mine).*

You will notice my emphasis here on the time word *then*. This rendering in the Revised Standard Version is undoubtedly an accurate translation of the Hebrew. It is somewhat different from the King James text, and may even create more problems, but it is certainly more true to the original. The amazing thing is that here we have the creation of man linked to the *third* day of creation when the land emerged from the seas and plant life began to appear.

The third and sixth days of creation, recorded in chapter one, are linked in a most unusual way. This present text supports the theory of a recapitulation: Days one, two, and three occur—and then, in a strange and remarkable way which no one fully understands, days four, five, and six occur and are individually linked with the first three days (day one with day four, two with five, three with six). Perhaps this opens the possibility of viewing these accounts of creation in a different light from the conventional six-day approach, and would account for the linking of man's creation with the third day.

It is also obvious that different conditions prevailed on earth at that time. There was no rain, but a mist watered the ground. It is possible that this condition continued until the flood; it may be that the rains that fell during the days of Noah were the first ever on earth, though geology would suggest otherwise. At least it is clear that conditions in the distant past were greatly different from today.

Man out of Dust

Next in the passage is this remarkable statement of the makeup of man:

> *Then the* LORD *God formed man of dust from the ground, and breathed into his nostrils the breath of life; and man became a living being [or, literally, a living soul] (Genesis 2:7).*

Here is a condensed account of tremendously significant things. We need not quibble over just how God formed man's body. Did he pile dirt together, wet it with water to make a mud statue, and then breathe life into it? No one knows. Perhaps the event occurred along the lines of the normal process of human birth. Certainly when we consider the miracle of conception, when two tiny, almost invisible cells meet and begin to grow and divide under a rigid interlock of controls, developing at last into a human being, we can't question God's ability to make man his own way. Nor should we be concerned about insignificant questions that prompted people in other times to beat each other over the head; whether Adam had a navel is not important. What we are told here, and what is important, is that God created man with three divisions.

God first made man's body, forming it from the dust of the earth. It is true that the same elements found in the dust of the ground are found also in our bodies. And it is to dust that we return.

You may recall the story of the little boy who came excitedly to his mother and said, "Mother, is it true that we are made from the dust and that after we die we go back to the dust?" She said, "Yes, it is." "Well," he said, "I looked under my bed this morning, and there's someone there either coming or going!"

We may not fully understand all that is involved in these pregnant phrases of Genesis 2:7, but it is important to notice that though the body of man was evidently formed first, the text itself does not say "the body," but rather that God formed *man* of dust from the earth. Man is more than a body. He is not merely an animated piece of beefsteak, a hunk of meat with a nervous system. He is more than body; he is soul as well. The functions of the soul are wonderfully linked to those of the body in ways we have not even begun to fathom.

For instance, the functions of the soul (reason, emotion, and will) are also in a remarkable way functions of our physical life. Reason is related to the brain, for it is only as the brain operates that reason occurs. Glands have great power over our emotional life. The hormones they secrete directly affect us emotionally. Thus the functions of the soul are tied to the body, and no one fully understands the mystery of it. In forming man, God made body and soul together, with the capacities for function of the soul lying dormant within the body.

Breath of Life

Then, into man's nostrils—into this body with an inactive soul—God breathed a living spirit. For the phrase "breath of life" in the Hebrew means a *spirit* of life. The words for breath and spirit are the same, both in Hebrew and in Greek, so that this is more than simply a picture of God breathing air into man's nostrils. This is not face-to-face resuscitation; it is the impartation of a spirit into man. As we know from other Scripture passages, the spirit is our essential nature. It is this that distinguishes man so remarkably from the animal creation. Thus man comes into being full-orbed, as a threefold being existing in body, soul and spirit.

Joining spirit and body activates and galvanizes the soul so it begins to function. Something of the same principle can be seen in an electric light bulb. By itself, a bulb is simply wire and glass, commonplace; but it has remarkable potential. Add an invisible substance—electricity—and pass it through that visible wire, and light is born. Light is different from the wire and different from the electricity, but it comes streaming forth from that bulb. It is much the same way with man. God made a body, with its possibilities of function as a soul, and breathed into it a spirit; the union of body and spirit produced the activity of soul, as light is produced from the wire and electricity.

When the spirit passes from the body, the body dies. James tells us, "The body apart from the spirit is dead" (James 2:26). We bury the body, and the spirit returns to the God who made it. Whatever portion of the soul which has been saved also returns with the spirit to God. It is significant that in the Scriptures the spirit is *regenerated* but the soul is *saved*. There is only one place in which Scripture ever mentions a spirit being saved, and there *spirit* seems to stand for both soul and spirit. It is the soul, the life we are living now, that needs to be saved. That part of it which is lived in the power of the Spirit of God, functioning in relationship to the Lord Jesus Christ as God intended man to live, is saved. Our souls are thus *being* saved as we live day by day in relationship to the Son of God. That saved soul, and only that, is what we have left after this life. All else is wood, hay, and stubble, to disappear in the judging flame of God.

Fallen man's spirit is dead. This is what Scripture means when it says man is dead in trespasses and sin. His spirit does not function as it should. Therefore the soul, which reflects like a mirror the activities of the spirit, is lifeless. This is what creates the intense, worldwide restlessness of our race, the inability to be satisfied, the unending search for answers that are never found. It is all an expression of a wasted spirit, lying ruined within us because of the fall of man. But in the beginning, as Adam came perfect from the hand of God, he was a lamp—and a lamp that was lit, alive in ways beyond anything that we can conjecture.

The third note of this passage is geographical:

> And the LORD God planted a garden in Eden,
> in the east; and there he put the man whom he

*had formed. And out of the ground the LORD
God made to grow every tree that is pleasant to
the sight and good for food, the tree of life also in
the midst of the garden, and the tree of the knowledge of good and evil.*

*A river flowed out of Eden to water the garden,
and there it divided and became four rivers. The
name of the first is Pishon; it is the one which
flows around the whole land of Havilah, where
there is gold; and the gold of that land is good;
bdellium and onyx stone are there. The name of
the second river is Gihon; it is the one which flows
around the whole land of Cush. And the name of
the third river is Tigris [or Hiddekel] which
flows east of Assyria. And the fourth river is the
Euphrates (Genesis 2:8-14).*

Here is the account of man placed in a garden. The
name of the garden is never given. It was not called
Eden; it was a garden placed in the land of Eden.
There is no suggestion here that the whole earth was
a garden as we sometimes mistakenly imagine. God
marked off a certain plot which he turned into a garden, and there he placed man. Man's task there was
to learn the secrets that would enable him to turn the
rest of the earth into a garden. But because man failed
in the garden, he was unable to discover those secrets,
and instead of turning the world into a garden he is
turning it into a garbage dump.

The proof that this account is no myth is that two
of the rivers mentioned can still be identified. Certain
geographical landmarks are given. Remember that
this account describes a place that existed before the
flood changed drastically the surface of the earth.
Still, the Tigris and Euphrates rivers bear those same
names today, and the other two rivers are perhaps

identical with two other streams that are still flowing, one into the Black Sea and the other into the Cas-
pian Sea. Both flow down from the mountains of
Ararat in Armenia, where the ark rested after the
flood.

There is an interesting reference here to the gold of
the land. If you are familiar with Greek mythology,
you know that the story of Jason and the Golden
Fleece is set in this same area. It was to this part of
the earth that Jason went in his search for the golden
fleece. Thus the idea of gold has been associated with
this land for a long time. The account is not myth,
but is grounded in history, as is all of Scripture. These
accounts are indeed symbolic, but they have roots sol-
idly grounded in fact.

The final and most important note is theological:

> The LORD God took the man and put him in the
> garden of Eden to till it and keep it. And the
> LORD God commanded the man, saying, "You
> may freely eat of every tree of the garden; but of
> the tree of the knowledge of good and evil you shall
> not eat, for in the day that you eat of it you shall
> die" (Genesis 2:15-17).

We must now take a look at these trees in the midst
of the garden. Once it was the fashion to deride this
account as ridiculous. The idea of Adam and Eve taking an actual fruit that had an evil effect upon them
has long been scorned. But in these days of increased
drug abuse we should hardly expect such disdain any
longer. Now we know all too well that drugs and substances taken from plants can be harmful. We know
that many of these substances are powerful, affecting
not only the human mind—stimulating it in
strange, mysterious, and even dangerous ways—but
also even the body's chromosome structure, thus pas-

sing along defects to children yet unborn. This is exactly the story of the garden of Eden.

Just as today we see young people drawn by the lure and attractiveness of the drug culture, so Eve was drawn to this strange and mysterious fruit that hung before her, enticing her with promises of extraordinary and wonderful things that would satisfy and fulfill her. She did not imagine that the actual partaking would damage and destroy the whole race that would follow. But what she did was *real*; this is no myth. We need struggle no longer with the literalness of this account.

After this brief appearance in Genesis, the tree of the knowledge of good and evil disappears from Scripture, primarily because its effects have become commonplace. But the tree of life appears again in the book of Revelation, conveying immortality and symbolizing the Lord Jesus Christ. In 2 Timothy 1:10, Paul said that Christ "abolished death and brought life and immortality to light through the gospel." As we come to the Lord Jesus Christ and are related to him, we receive the gift promised by this tree of life in the garden of Eden—the fruit from which man was once excluded.

What Is This Tree?

But what is this tree of the knowledge of good and evil? That question looms before us as we look at this chapter. After all, what is wrong with knowing good and evil? Surely it is a good thing to know the difference! Many Scripture passages encourage us to become mature enough to distinguish between the two, and one mark of immaturity in a Christian is that he cannot tell the difference. He is like a child, like a worldling; he cannot tell good from evil. But if it is a good thing to know the difference, why did

God forbid Adam to partake of this fruit?

We understand a little more if we look ahead to chapter 3, where in the story of man's fall we have the serpent's words to the woman:

> *For God knows that when you eat of it your eyes will be opened, and you will be like God, knowing good and evil (Genesis 3:5).*

Remember that not everything the devil says is a lie. He misuses truth in order to draw us on until we become the victims of his lie. He baits his trap with truth, and here is the truth from the lips of the devil: "You will have your eyes opened when you eat of this fruit, and you will be like God, knowing good and evil." These words suggest a clue as to what this fruit was and what it did.

How does God know good and evil? Think about it for a moment and you will see that God knows evil not by experience (because he cannot experience evil), but by relating it to himself. That which is consistent with his character and his nature is good; that which is inconsistent with it is evil. That which is out of line, out of character with himself, is evil, destructive, and dangerous; but all that is in line with his own nature is good. This is how God "knows" good and evil. He distinguishes it by himself.

It Was All a Lie

But only God can properly do this. In all the universe, only God has this right to define good and evil in relation to himself. Anyone else who tries it gets into trouble. The creatures of God's universe are made to discover the difference between good and evil by relating everything to God, not to themselves. When man ate of the fruit he began to do what God does—to relate everything to himself. Yet as a creature, he had no real ability to maintain this kind of relationship, and thus he interjected an unbalanced element into life. When man began to think of himself as the center of the universe, he became like God. But it was all a lie. Man is not the center of the universe, and cannot be.

As you trace the course of human history you can see this seductive lie which the serpent has whispered into human ears ever since: "*You* are the center of life. This is *your* world; everything relates to *you*. What you like is right; what you don't like is wrong. What you want to do is right; don't let anyone make you do what you don't want to do. You are the center of things." You can find this idea throbbing and pulsating throughout man-made philosophies, and even in television commercials, that man stands at the center of things.

This is the curse that fell on Adam when he ate of the fruit in the garden of Eden. His mind was twisted and he thought of himself as God, relating all things to himself. But this thinking introduced an eccentric element into creation, and our problem today is that we have an earth filled with billions of such eccentrics! This is why everything is always going off in wrong directions.

But the glory of the gospel is that when we are redeemed through faith in Jesus Christ we resume a balanced life, and everything relates once again to God. God now becomes the center of things. Though we may struggle to learn this, eventually all the thrust of the gospel affects us, putting God back into the center of his world and relating everything in our lives to him and not to us. It does not make any difference how things around us affect us. The important thing is, What do they do to God? What is his relationship to these things?

Let me illustrate with two stories from Guatemala. Some friends and I were driving in that country's old capital city, Antigua, with its lush tropical vegetation and its marvelous setting at the foot of three volcanoes. As we went about the city, they told me these two stories:

Several years ago, a mutual friend of ours named Dick had been killed in an automobile accident. Investigators at the scene had observed that Dick and another man in the car, Victor, had not fastened their seat belts. One of the investigators, an expert in this field, had commented that if their seat belts had been fastened, Victor would have been killed instead of Dick.

When this was told to Dick's widow, her response was to cry out, "Why did this happen? Why was Dick chosen? Why did he have to die?" But later, as she watched Victor in his ministry and saw how he was used and what a blessing he was to so many—though she knew her husband was equally gifted—she faced this question and found there was only one answer: God. It was God's choice, God's will. She said, "Who am I to tell him who to choose? God has the right to make these decisions." Thus she related the most tragic event of her life to the central Being of history, and found peace for her troubled heart.

The other story concerned Cameron Townsend, founder of Wycliffe Bible Translators. He came as a man of twenty-one into the high mountains of Guatemala near Lake Atitlan and there began his translation work. From that simple beginning the worldwide ministry of Wycliffe Bible Translators has come. At Wycliffe's fiftieth anniversary celebration in Guatemala, Cameron Townsend was highly honored by the government and people of Guatemala and other nations in Central America. They had banquet after banquet in his name, and he was given the highest honors those countries could bestow. Everywhere he went he was feted and his work exalted.

But my friend told me that, typically, Dr. Townsend turned every occasion into an opportunity to speak of the Lord Jesus Christ and of his work. Refusing the honor for himself, he related it to the One to whom it belonged. He put God into the center of things and maintained the balance of life.

This is what Scripture means when it says that all of life must be built around the Lord Jesus in order to make sense. A day is coming when every knee shall bow and every tongue confess that Jesus is Lord to the glory of God the Father. Then the destruction, desolation, and heartache of the garden of Eden will be reversed, and men will once again acknowledge the centrality of God in life. The world will be filled with glory and righteousness, from the River to the ends of the earth. Everything will be what God intended it to be.

But the glory of the gospel is that this can happen in human hearts *right now*. This is what the gospel message is all about. Have you ceased your rebellion against the will of God? Have you stopped trying to be a little god, trying to run things in your own home or office the way you want them to be? Have you crowned Jesus Christ Lord of his empire, and gladly invited him to sit on the throne of your heart and rule there, where he belongs? Have you stopped your grumbling and complaining about all the things he has chosen to come into your life? Have you instead begun to rejoice as 1 Thessalonians 5:18 exhorts us, "Give thanks in all circumstances; for this is the will of God in Christ Jesus for you"?

We need this exhortation to remind us of one great theme: Life cannot and will not make sense, and it will not cease its endless friction, until it is related to Jesus Christ our Lord. Only by crowning him anew each day as Lord of lords and King of kings will we find peace. To live each day in this holy relationship—is life!

3
THE MAKING OF WOMAN

As a man who lived for years with a wife, four daughters and a mother-in-law, I approach the subject of understanding women with considerable timidity. At our home, I'm even grateful for a *mailbox* out front!

In exploring this subject, however, we must turn not to experience but to the wonderfully helpful words of Scripture. The latter part of Genesis 2 tells of woman's creation and of her role in marriage—for when God made woman, marriage was born.

In these latitudinarian days we read occasionally of the "marriage" of homosexuals. What a shabby, pathetic imitation of what God intended marriage to be! Marriage involves a man and a woman, and this passage reveals to us three very helpful things relating to women and to marriage. First we see God's intent in making woman, then a significant description of the process he used, and finally an ouline of the qualities of true marriage

Let us first turn to God's intent:

> Then the LORD God said, "It is not good that the man should be alone; I will make him a helper fit for him." So out of the ground the LORD God formed every beast of the field and every bird of the air, and brought them to the man to see what he would call them; and whatever the man called every living creature, that was its name. The man gave names to all cattle, and to the birds of the air, and to every beast of the field; but for the man there was not found a helper fit for him (2:18-20).

The first thing this passage makes clear is that woman was made to be man's *companion*. "It is not good that the man should be alone." One of the most shattering emotions human beings can experience is loneliness. When God pronounced a sentence of "not good" upon man's condition, it was the first negative pronouncement in the story of creation. Until then, everything had been declared good, and on the sixth day of creation God said that everything he had done was "very good." But now we read that it was not good for man to be alone, indicating that it never was God's intention for man to be alone. From the very beginning he intended to make two sexes.

Loneliness is always a devastating threat to happiness and welfare. Loneliness is now reckoned to be the single greatest cause of suicide in this country, and it is undoubtedly the most widespread source of human misery today. Yet it is a perfectly human experience. Each of us has felt at times the need for human companionship. There is nothing wrong with that; God made us that way. We need one another. We were not made to exist in solitude.

Drawing from the closing words of Paul's second letter to Timothy, John R. W. Stott once described how lonely the great apostle had become. Stott pictured the apostle as he sat in his tiny dungeon in Rome, with a circular opening in the ceiling above him as the only access, and how he wrote to Timothy that all had forsaken him. He begged the young man to come to him soon, before winter if possible, and to bring with him certain articles of clothing, books, and parchments, because he was cold in body, bored in mind, and lonely in spirit. Stott brought out what a perfectly human reaction this was. Despite the fact that the apostle could look beyond this life—that his departure was near at hand, that he was about to join the Lord in glory—and though he was thrilled with the possibilities opening before him, yet this did not cancel out the human element of loneliness.

God knows we need one another, and he provides others for us. It is clear from Genesis 2 that the chief answer—though not the sole answer—to man's loneliness is the making of woman. One of the primary purposes of marriage is to provide companionship, a sharing of life together. I've read that one of the famous actresses of the stage, the skilled and popular Gertrude Lawrence, once announced to her friends that she would like to get married. "Why?" they asked. "You have everything anyone could want: fame, close friends, abundant social life. What could marriage add to you?" She answered, "I want so

desperately to have someone to nudge." Her response
highlighted the need for companionship, this
elementary human hunger.

Designed to Help

Second, God intended that woman should be a
helper to man, sharing not only his life but his work
and responsibilities as well. Man and woman are to
work together in building a home and a life. This has
been true from the very beginning; men and women
are designed to work together. Perhaps there is nothing more destructive to marriage than the commonly
held attitude that the man has his own area of responsibility, his realm of life, his work—and the woman
has hers, with little or no sharing between them. It is
always destructive in any home or marriage for one
mate to hold out a private realm that excludes the
other. It is terribly wrong, for example, for the man
to have nothing much to say when he is home, and
the woman to have nothing to do with her husband's
work.

It is clear from this passage that God made woman
to be man's helper and to share his responsibility,
though they may have different assignments according to the nature of their work. There is an aspect of
responsibility falling primarily upon the husband,
but the decisionmaking and labor involved in the
marriage and home and family are to be shared
equally by husband and wife. This is made clear in
this reference to woman as man's helper. But it is
made even clearer by the remarkable verse that follows.

Here we have what logicians might be tempted to
call a *non sequitur*, something which appears to have
no relationship to what has gone before; it does not
seem to follow. We have just read that God intends to

make "*a helper fit for him,*" which of course must be a woman. Then we read:

> *So out of the ground the* LORD *God formed every beast of the field and every bird of the air, and brought them to the man to see what he would call them; and whatever the man called every living creature, that was its name (2:19).*

What has this to do with making a woman? How does it follow God's declaration of intent to make a helper for man? Obviously there must be a connection. God set Adam to the task of studying the animals in order to name them. He gave him a project to carry out before he was ready for marriage. Doubtless it was to show him that his wife would be quite different from the animals. Many men have not learned that yet, but it is clear that this was God's intent in sending man on this search.

What did he learn as he examined the animals? Adam could not have given names to the beasts without knowing the character of each, because a name always reflects a characteristic. To name each animal, Adam had to understand—whether through reason or by a revelation from God—something of the character of each animal. Adam learned several things immediately.

Pertaining to Animals

Perhaps he learned first that woman was not to be a mere beast of burden, as she has so often become in the history of the race since. There are societies where women are treated exactly like animals, where the price of a woman is approximately the price of a cow, and where women are sometimes traded for cows. But this violates what Adam learned in the beginning: Woman is *not* like the animals. Adam did not find in the animals a helper fit for him. His wife, when she appeared, was to be quite different.

Therefore woman is not to be treated as a slave whose function begins and ends with household work. A woman's personality is devastated when her husband treats her as though she were only a servant or housekeeper, existing only to keep everything in order. Perhaps the most frequent complaint from married women is a variation on the theme: "He looks upon me just like another thing around the house. I'm like part of the furniture." This is terribly destructive to a woman's psychological makeup.

Second, Adam unquestionably learned in his search that woman is not to be merely a biological laboratory for producing children. Obviously it is women who bear children, but they are not to be like the animals who bear progeny as almost their sole reason for existence. Sex has a much higher function in human life than mere reproduction. One of the most destructive ideas spread among mankind has been that the first and primary reason for marriage is the production of children. The Bible does not say that at all. The Bible gives ample justification for birth control when circumstances warrant, and we have come to understand this under the terrible pressure of an exploding population. Woman was never intended to be merely a baby factory, for she was not like the animals.

Third, Adam probably learned in his search that woman is not a "thing" outside himself. Women are not beasts of burden, they are not simply for producing children, and they are not something to be used at a man's whim and then disposed of. Woman is a helper fit for him, corresponding to him. Many modern philosophies of life declare women to be nothing more than playthings for men. They are disposable women—you use them as you would use a Kleenex, and then toss them away. But this passage directly contradicts that. Woman is to be a helper and a companion, fit for man, corresponding exactly and continuously to him, constantly able to adjust to the changes that come into his life.

Let us move on to consider briefly the process God followed in making woman:

> *So the LORD God caused a deep sleep to fall upon the man, and while he slept took one of his ribs and closed up its place with flesh; and the rib which the LORD God had taken from the man he made into a woman and brought her to the man (2:21-22).*

This account has been derided and scorned as impossible, yet those who deride it forget that they are reckoning with an almighty God. A scientist once told me that it is theoretically possible for any cell of the body to reproduce, not only itself and the member of which it is a part, but ultimately the whole body. Whether or not this is possible, there can be no problem in God taking an actual rib and using it to make a woman. It is absurd to argue (as some do) that this could not have happened because men have the same number of ribs as do women. If you cut off your finger, it does not mean that your children will be born minus one digit.

Two things about this are significant. First, we are told man was caused to fall into a deep sleep and that woman was made during this period of unconsciousness. These things suggest certain continuing relationships. This period of unconsciousness strongly suggests what modern psychology also confirms, that the marriage relationship—the ties between a man and his wife—are far deeper than mere surface affection. They are a part not only of man's conscious life, but also of his subconscious.

This explains what any marriage counselor soon recognizes: why it is that men and women can be so puzzled by one another's reactions. They know that they themselves are upset or angry or hurt at something the other one has done, but they can't put their finger on the reason. It is, of course, because the other person has violated a basic drive which God himself built into the masculine or feminine nature. Though we cannot put our finger on what is bothering us, we know there is something wrong.

This is why Peter in his first letter exhorts the man to dwell with his wife "according to knowledge" (1 Peter 3:7, KJV). The responsibility of the man in marriage is to understand what the Scriptures teach about women, and to help his wife understand herself as well as to understand him. She will have a much easier task understanding him than she does herself.

Close to the Heart

The second revelation here is that woman was made from a rib. Skeptics laugh at this, but God knew what he was doing. It is significant that a rib was chosen. The rib emphasizes the essentially emotional nature of women. Ribs are the bones nearest the heart, and are thus closely linked with the heart. Throughout Scripture the heart is always pictured as the center of emotional life.

Modern psychology confirms this emotional character of woman. Tears, fears, and cheers often come more easily to women than to men. In this, woman is designed to complete man, to be a helper fit for him. It is this very emotional nature which adds color and warmth to life. How drab life would be without it!

The second significant aspect of the rib is that it emphasizes the protective instinct in women. It is the rib which protects the vital organs of the chest, and notably the heart. In fact, the Hebrew word for "helper" is the word *azar*, which means "to surround." Just as the rib cage surrounds the heart and protects it, so woman are instinctively protective. Anyone who has tried to come between a man and his wife, or to abuse a man to his wife, knows what I mean. C. S. Lewis pointed this out in asking, "If your dog has bitten a neighbor's child, would you rather face the mother or the father to discuss the issue?"

So God's process in making woman reveals that she is to be a companion and a helper, utilizing to the full her inherent emotional and protective instincts. Now we come to the qualities of marriage that result from the union of man and woman:

> Then the man said, "This at last is bone of my bones and flesh of my flesh; she shall be called Woman, because she was taken out of Man." Therefore a man leaves his father and his mother and cleaves to his wife, and they become one flesh. And the man and his wife were both naked, and were not ashamed (2:23-25).

This is a remarkable passage because it encompasses in brief all the great concepts of marriage that run throughout the rest of the Bible. They are condensed and encapsulated in these few verses. When God had finished making woman, and Adam had slept off the deep unconsciousness into which he had fallen, God brought the woman to Adam. What a scene that must have been! Here is the first of a long, long series of boy-meets-girl stories. Out of the highly condensed account of this encounter there emerge four factors essential to true marriage.

One Flesh

The first and most fundamental is that marriage is
to involve a complete identity of the partners; two are
to be one. Adam's first reaction when he saw his wife
was, "This at last is bone of my bones and flesh of my
flesh"; that is, *She is one being with me.* This is
strengthened in the latter part of verse 24: "and they
will become one flesh." It is not without reason that
this recognition of unity has become part of the marriage service. As someone has well said, the one word
above all that makes marriage successful is "ours."
Things belong to "us." "Bone of my bones and flesh
of my flesh." Thus, as the New Testament so wisely
points out, the man who hurts his wife is hurting
himself. He may not feel it directly, but down the
line it will show in his own life, because she is really,
genuinely, and factually sharing one life with him.
They become one flesh. This is not poetry; it is reality.

Two people become one when they are married,
and as their life goes on together, there is a blending
of psyches, a merging of lives, and the creating of a
single history. It is for this reason that divorce is such
a terrible thing, especially after years of marriage. It
is the severing of a person. It is butchery, the dividing
up of a single life, much as you would take an axe and
split a body in two. No wonder it is so terribly painful—much more deeply felt than those who experience it understand at the time.

The second thing mentioned here is the biblical
principle of headship, which is developed at much
greater length in the New Testament. "She shall be
called woman, because she was taken out of man."
Paul enlarges on this in his letter to the Corinthians,
pointing out that man was not made for woman but
woman was made for man (1 Corinthians 11:9). It is

the man who is ultimately responsible before God for the nature and character of the home. It is the man who must lead in determining the direction of the home, and must therefore answer for that leadership (or its lack) before God. The woman's responsibility is to acknowledge this leadership.

One of the most serious threats to marriage and one of the primary causes of divorce today is that men are abdicating their leadership of the home, leaving it up to the wife to rear the children. They refuse to be fathers to their children and husbands to their wives, wanting rather to be sons to another mother and to have their own needs met.

Third, the passage teaches that marriage is permanent. "Therefore a man leaves his father and his mother and cleaves to his wife." This word "cleaves" is a strong word. In the Hebrew it is *dabag*, which means "to adhere firmly, as if with glue," to be lovingly devoted to a wife. In the days of the Model T, someone asked Henry Ford what accounted for his successful marriage. He said, "The same formula as the making of a successful car: Stick to one model." That is exactly what this passage says. A husband is to cleave to his wife. He forsakes all others and adheres to her. Whatever she may be like, he is to cleave to her. He is to stay with her, and she with him, because marriage is permanent.

Nothing to Hide

Finally, the fourth factor: "And the man and his wife were both naked, and were not ashamed." This describes the openness between a man and wife—literally, nothing to hide. They have no secrets, nothing that they do not share with each other. It is the failure to achieve this kind of openness that lies behind so many marriage breakdowns—the utter lack of communication. Two sit and look at one another and say nothing. They may talk about trivialities, but they do not discuss their problems or what they are thinking. This is often why they are so judgmental with one another, each one trying to get the other to agree, being unwilling to allow differences of opinion.

But openness does not mean agreeing or feeling the same. It means a readiness to share with one another, completely, without insisting that the other adopt the same attitude. There is room here for ultimate decisions and the submitting of a wife to the leadership of the husband. Openness does not cancel that out. But there is to be a complete freedom of communication, one with the other. Marriages shrivel, wither, and die when this is not true.

What is the result of all this? In Eden all these principles were at work. Adam and Eve were united as one. They recognized the principle of headship. Adam had the right to make ultimate decisions in all matters. They intended to be together permanently and Adam was responsible for this. There was an openness between them so that they hid nothing from one another. What was the result? The text says, "They were not ashamed." What were they, then, if not ashamed? What is the opposite of being ashamed? It is to be relaxed. We would use the term "well adjusted." They felt at ease with each other. There was no strain in their marriage. They were fully at ease with one another.

Isn't this what we strive for in marriage? Here in Genesis 2 are the principles that produce it. Here is God's design.

As we hold it before us, we can see by contrast why so many marriages fail today. We need desperately to return to this biblical pattern, for here are revealed the secrets of happy married life.

4
THE
ENTICEMENT
OF EVIL

We come to Genesis 3 with a heightened sense of anticipation. In many ways this is the most important information ever conveyed to mankind.

Here is the ultimate explanation for the tensions and conflicts that constantly flare up around the world. Here we have the answer to the eternal "why" that arises in times of tragedy or sorrow. Here is the explanation for more than a hundred centuries of heartache, misery, torture, blood, sweat, and tears. Here is the reason for the powerful fascination that drugs hold for young people today, as well as the secrets of our passion for power, and the lure of wealth, and the enticements of forbidden sex to young and old alike. Here is the only reasonable answer for the existence of all these things.

Remove this chapter from the Bible and the rest of it is incomprehensible. Ignore the teaching of this chapter, and the story of humanity becomes impossible to understand or explain.

The most striking thing about Genesis 3 is that you and I find ourselves here. You can't read this story without feeling you have lived it yourself . . . because you have.

The Temptation and the Fall are reproduced in our lives many times a day. We have all heard the voice of the tempter. We have all felt the drawing of sin. We know the pangs of guilt that follow.

This is why many call this story a *myth*. In the sense that this story contains timeless truth, perhaps the word *myth* has certain rationality. But there are other implications of the term that make it unsuitable for this account. Genesis 3 is timeless in that the same experience is always happening to mankind, but it is also timeless because it is fact. It actually did occur. It happens continually because it did happen once to our original parents; because it happened once, we, their children, cannot escape repeating it. In that sense there is no chapter in the Bible more up-to-date and more pertinent to our own situation than this one.

This chapter also tells us that the serpent was "more subtle than any other wild creature." The word *subtle* means crafty or cunning. His craftiness is evident right from the beginning in that he sought out the woman. A desire to play on her emotional nature led the devil to seek out the woman and to begin his temptation with her.

He comes, as he always does, in disguise. He never appears with horns, hooves, and a tail, announcing that he is Satan. If he did, everyone would reject him. Few of us want to submit to evil in that open, defiant way. But the devil is disguised, appearing not bad but good, with a wholesome character and benevolent purpose. The disguise he chose was that of a serpent, a creature whose Hebrew name meant "shining one"; he was a creature of beauty and attractiveness.

The Devil Is Limited

Let us move on to consider the strategy the tempter employs. It is exactly the same strategy he uses on us. The personality he exemplifies and the character in which he appears are the same now as then. Scripture makes clear that the devil can also appear as a roaring lion; he can strike in tragedy and sickness and physical evil, as he did to Job or to the apostle Paul with his thorn in the flesh (which Paul called the messenger of Satan). Or, as a lion, he can strike fear into our hearts. But his most effective strategy is to appear as an angel of light. As such, his strategy is always the same.

Actually, this should be encouraging. If you learn how to recognize the devil's strategy, you will find that he invariably employs the same tactics. In a sense the devil is very limited. He doesn't vary his tactics widely. Sometimes we feel we will never learn how to anticipate the devil. But we can learn. The apostle Paul said he was not ignorant of the devil's devices. If we learn how Satan works, we can easily detect him in our lives.

The apostle James has described the devil's strategy plainly:

> *Each person is tempted when he is lured and enticed by his own desire. Then desire when it has conceived gives birth to sin; and sin when it is full-grown brings forth death (James 1:14-15).*

This was the devil's strategy in the garden of Eden and it is his strategy in your life and mine. The only difference between us and Eve in the garden is that for her the tempter stood outside her. She was innocent and he stood outside attempting to reach into her mind and thoughts. Since mankind's fall, the tempter speaks within us and has access to us so that we are never out of reach of his temptation. We are always exposed. We can go a thousand miles away but we will never be able to avoid temptation. Wherever we go we carry within us a tempter, which the New Testament calls *the flesh*.

Yet he always approaches us in the same three stages outlined in this passage from James. His first tactic is to arouse desire. James says that every man "is tempted when he is lured and enticed by his own desire." The first step the devil takes is always to arouse our desire to do wrong, to create a hunger, a lure or enticement toward evil. The second is to permit intent to form and an act to occur. As James describes it, "Desire when it has conceived gives birth to sin."

Notice that James employs the symbol of conception and birth. There is a gestation period in temptation, for once desire is aroused a process occurs which sooner or later issues in sin, a wrong act. In the third stage the devil immediately moves in to produce what Scripture describes as death. "Sin when it is full-grown brings forth death."

This is the devil's ultimate aim. Jesus said that Satan was a murderer from the beginning. He delights in mangling, smashing, twisting, destroying, blighting, and blasting. We can see his activity everywhere. It goes on all around us, in our own lives and in the lives of others. These are "the works of the devil," says Scripture. He brings them about by the process we see in this story.

Let us watch how the tempter moves cunningly to arouse desire in Eve's heart.

> *He said to the woman, "Did God say, 'You shall not eat of any tree of the garden'?" And the woman said to the serpent, "We may eat of the fruit of the trees of the garden; but God said, 'You shall not eat of the fruit of tree which is in the midst of the garden, neither shall you touch it, lest you die.'" But the serpent said to the woman, "You will not die. For God knows that when you eat of it your eyes will be opened, and you will be like God, knowing good and evil" (3:1-5).*

His first task is to make the woman want to sin. This is not very difficult with us. We respond quite readily to these desires, these urges to do wrong. But it was quite different with Eve. Remember, at this time she was innocent, and she trusted and loved God. She felt no wrong desire springing up within her, such as we must wrestle with. The tempter had to awaken a wrong desire. His opportunity was provided by the free will God gave to mankind. This helps explain an often asked question: How is it that the devil was allowed access to the garden of Eden in the first place? Why does the tempter appear in this story? How did he get into the garden?

The only possible answer is that God allowed him to come in. He was permitted to come. He came with the full knowledge and consent of God, for it was necessary that man be tempted. Man must be able to respond *voluntarily* to God. The greatest gift God has given to us is the ability to make moral choices; we have the right to be wrong if we insist. God himself does not violate this. He does not coerce us. He does not force us to be right. We have the right to reject his love, and the right to turn off his grace, refuse his mercy, and go our own stubborn way. God allows that to be. It is the greatest dignity given to man.

Many people struggle with this. They ask, "Why doesn't God make us behave?" But if he did, he would have taken away this greatest dignity. These same people will say, "I don't want anyone telling me what to do. I want to make up my own mind." You can't have it both ways. Since God is a God of love—and love never coerces, never forces someone to love in return—it is essential that man be given the chance to choose whether he wants to continue to love God or to go another direction. So because of the gift of free will, the tempter comes into the garden and is given the opportunity to tempt the woman. Free will makes us men, but it also makes us temptable. Even the Lord Jesus faced this trial. He too was given the gift of free choice, and was therefore exposed to the power of Satan.

Seed of Doubt

Notice that in trying to arouse desire in this woman the tempter follows a threefold plan—the same way in which he will move with us. His first step was to implant in her heart a distrust of God's love. He raised the question, "Did God say you shall not eat of any tree of the garden?" He meant by this, "Could God have said a thing like that, really? How well do you know him? Do you think a God who loves you would ask you not to eat of a tree in this garden?"

With that question he plants a seed of doubt in the woman's mind. He is seeking to alter the image of God in her thinking. He is saying in effect, "Either you misunderstood him and he didn't really say that, or if he did say it, he obviously is not quite the kind of God you have imagined him to be." With this single question he casts a small cloud over Eve's trust in God and the response of love in her heart. Could God really have said a thing like that?

Have you ever heard this question? Can a God who loves you forbid anything to you? Is it really love if he forbids something? The question hangs over the whole human race and has done so ever since this first occasion in the garden.

You will notice that the woman's answer is perfectly forthright, without guile. She says immediately,

> *We may eat of the fruit of the trees of the garden;*
> *but God said, 'You shall not eat of the fruit of the*
> *tree which is in the midst of the garden, neither*
> *shall you touch it, lest you die.'"*

Some have accused the woman of adding to God's statement when she says, "Neither shall you touch it," because that was not part of the prohibition given in verse seventeen of chapter two. I do not think we need to view it that way. Perhaps the woman is giving a fuller account of what God had said; perhaps he said, "Look, this tree is harmful and therefore don't go near it. Don't expose yourself to its temptation."

In the Lord's Prayer we are taught to pray, "Lead us not into temptation." Notice the prayer does not say, "Lead me out of temptation once I have gotten into it." No, by the time we have gotten into it, we are already half lost. When we feel the raging of desire within us, it is a late hour to start praying. The Lord teaches us to pray beforehand, "Lead me not even into the realm of temptation. Don't let me come to the place where I shall feel this tremendous arousing and awakening of desire within."

Point of Limitation

Notice that temptation always comes to us at this point of limitation. God said to the man and the woman, "Here is an area in which I must limit you. There is only this one place. The whole world is yours, this entire planet. You may eat of any fruit, any tree, anywhere—except for this one." Haven't you discovered that God is forever saying this to us also, in one way or another? In this sense, the tree of good and evil is still right in the midst of the garden of our lives. Wherever we may turn we are confronted by the fact that we are limited in some way. The testing of our humanity is whether we are willing to accept and abide by the limitations God puts upon us.

As a child, are you willing to accept the authority of your parents in the home? As a student, are you willing to accept that you are not a mature person yet, that you are still learning the rules of life and can't make them up yourself? As a wife, are you willing to accept the authority of your husband? Are you willing to recognize that *God* has made a distinction between the sexes and that the husband is given a role of leadership that the wife does not have? As a man or woman, are you willing to accept that you are a created human being, and not God—that there are things you cannot know and mysteries which you can't explore? These are some of the testing points in your life.

You are not an infinite being; you are finite. You don't know everything. You must sit at the feet of God and listen to his voice and learn from him. You are not equipped with all it takes to explore life adequately. You are man. Are you willing to accept that limitation? Throughout the whole history of our race the violation of this limitation has brought sorrow, heartache, and misery.

Now see how the tempter moves in quickly. He dares to deny openly the results God said would follow disobedience. "You will not die," he declares. He openly substitutes a lie for the truth, but he does it in the realm of the future where you can't check the results beforehand. Notice his cleverness as he says, "It is not going to happen as God says. Don't take God so seriously. Surely these issues are not that important. If God is a God of love, then this can't be a life-or-death matter. Don't make a federal case out of this! It is really trivial."

Do you see how this is repeated in life today? It is so easy to say, "These things are simple matters which deal only with secondary issues. This is not what the Bible says it is—a life-or-death matter—at least you can't take it that way if you believe in a God who loves you." So the devil cleverly uses the great truths about God's character to plant a doubt in this woman's heart, and to support it with an outright lie, declaring that what God had warned of would not happen.

Then comes the third step. Quickly he moves in to support his lie with a distorted truth. If we look closely at the many cults of our day, we can see that every false faith is made up of a certain amount of truth—ten percent error and ninety percent truth, mixed together. Ultimately the ten percent of error leads men astray. This is exactly the devil's tactic here. He said to Eve,

> *God knows that when you eat of it your eyes will be opened, and you will be like God, knowing good and evil.*

This was perfectly true. Look at verse 7: "Then the eyes of both were opened." And at verse 22: "Then the LORD God said, 'Behold, the man has become like one of us, knowing good and evil.'"

This is exactly what the devil said would happen—
but with this difference: Though their eyes *were*
opened and they *did* become able to know good and
evil as God knows it—they learned to relate everything to themselves. To measure good and evil they
used their own feelings. This is also what God does,
but the devil didn't tell them this would be the most
disastrous thing possible. They thought the devil
meant something expansive, something glorious.
But when their eyes were opened it was shameful, sor-
did, and sad. "Oh," you say, "how diabolically
clever." Exactly! This is the way the devil always
works. Eyes are opened . . . but not to what is ex-
pected.

The devil now is through with the woman. He has
succeeded in arousing desire, and this is all he wants.
The other two stages will almost certainly follow, and
they do, for Eve is now deceived. All the devil wishes
to do or needs to do is to leave Eve standing before the
fruit, hanging there in all its luscious fascination,
tantalizing her, offering her an experience she never
dreamed possible. He has planted his vile seed. He
has caused her to slightly distrust God's love, to believe a lie, and to expect an unwarranted result. She
stands aroused and deceived, in the presence of the
fruit, and the devil can safely leave her even though
she has not yet sinned. He is fully certain that the desired results will follow.

"What went wrong here?" you ask. "How could
she have avoided this? Where was the battle lost?" As
you look through the account you can see the battle
was lost right after the first sentence, after Satan
raised the question, "Did God say . . .?" From the
moment Eve mentally accepted the idea that God was
not fully to be trusted, she was whipped, beaten, and

lost. Immediately the devil became bold and lied to her blatantly. And she believed him from then on.

Have you experienced this kind of thing? This is the process the tempter uses when he tries to get you to have an affair with another man's wife or another woman's husband. This is the process he follows when he wants to get you involved in a shady business deal, or to cheat on an examination, or simply to tell a lie (even a little "white" one).

God's Way—Satan's Way

The interesting thing about this is that there was nothing wrong in arousing desire in this woman's heart, because God does that too. God is at work to arouse our desires, to make us want to do his will, to stimulate us and activate us, to move us. The difference is in how each of them does it. If we get nothing else out of this story, we will have learned a tremendous lesson if we can differentiate between how God arouses desire and how the devil arouses desire.

How does God do it? First, he demonstrates his love to us. This is always God's first approach. He comes and touches us somehow, blesses us, pours out upon us his sunshine and his rain, all the blessings of our lives. He comes in Christ and moves among us and lives with us, blessing us. He gives himself.

Second, he declares a promised result. He gives his word to us. He declares what will happen. He opens to us a new vista of what life can be like.

Third, he offers us his presence to bring about the fulfillment of that promise. Jesus said, "Come unto me," and "If any one hears my voice and opens the door, I will come in to him" (Revelation 3:20). God offers to enter life personally and to be with us. This leads to fulfillment, blessing, joy, and oneness.

Do you see the contrast between the way God works and the way the devil works? The devil first implants a distrust of God's love; the Lord *demonstrates* his love. God *declares* a promise to us; the devil declares a countering lie. God strengthens his promise by offering himself, the truth itself, to us. The devil distorts that truth and makes it look like something else, makes it vague and undefined. This is how you can tell the difference.

Are you being tempted to do wrong, to take a course that is wrong, to make a decision that will lead to death or disaster down the line? How do you know whether it is from God or Satan? It all looks so good, doesn't it? Then ask yourself these questions: Do I feel cheated, deprived, or limited right now? Do I feel as though God is somehow holding out on me, that I am not being given all that I ought to have, that my rights are being violated, that I am being cheated of something life should give me? If I feel this way, I am listening to the voice of the tempter. This is his first approach. "Did God say this? Would a God who loves you say a thing like that? Would he hold out on you? Would he postpone the blessing he wants you to have?"

Then ask yourself if what you want contradicts the truth God has revealed. Can you find in Scripture that what you seek is wrong, yet all the world is telling you it is right and will bring you blessing? Does the word of God stand in opposition to what you are after? Then you are listening again to the tempter's voice, for he lies, outrightly, blatantly. He says the results will be different from what God's revealed word says.

Finally ask yourself if the promised result is rather vague and uncertain. Is it just a general promise of blessing or happiness, or is it specific—clearly and precisely defined? If it is unspecific, you are listening again to the voice of the tempter. This is why Scripture comes back again and again to this simple theme:

> *Trust in the LORD with all your heart, and do*
> *not rely on your own insight (Proverbs 3:5).*

We are but men and women, only human. We don't know all there is to know about life. We can't know. There isn't anyone who knows. We desperately need the truth that comes from God alone. No one else can supply it. No other book will give us the answers. There is no other place to find out what life is all about except in God's word.

Therefore, "Trust in the LORD with all your heart, and do not rely on your own insight. In all your ways acknowledge him, and he will make straight your paths" (Proverbs 3:5-6).

5
THE HEART
OF TEMPTATION

We have watched Eve in the garden of Eden being assaulted in mind and will, as the tempter sought to arouse her desire for the forbidden fruit. Temptation always pressures us to exceed the limitations which God has established. God has set these limitations not out of cruelty or unkindness, but out of love and grace. They are necessary to our humanity. But the character of temptation is to make us distrust this limitation, to make us restive and discontented so we will exceed the limits.

With Eve, the tempter accomplished this by first creating within her a sense of unfairness. We see the same thing today. Many are seething in a ferment of discontent and restlessness, suffering (often justifiably) from a sense of being treated unfairly, and allowing resentment to take control. The tempter did that with Eve. Eve's mind, which began to believe God had been unjust, was prepared to believe God is not trustworthy and does not really love. The third step was to give her an incomplete and misleading statement of truth; to twist it, distort it slightly. Thus her desire was aroused for the forbidden fruit, and she was ready to act.

Now stage two occurs. In many ways this is the most important of all. Before it was reached Eve could have resisted the temptation aroused within her, but after this point it becomes more difficult—in fact, practically impossible. This stage is given in verse 6:

> *So when the woman saw that the tree was good*
> *for food, and that it was a delight to the eyes,*
> *and that the tree was desired to make one wise,*
> *she took of its fruit and ate; and she also gave*
> *some to her husband, and he ate.*

Up to now the tempter had worked upon Eve's feelings to arouse a strong desire within her for the forbidden thing. But now the mind must come into action. It is the function of the mind to judge the logic of a situation.

Our mental faculties are a tremendous gift from God. They reflect on circumstances and facts, and relate our attitude or activity to these. A certain logic must prevail. The question of the mind is always: Is the action about to be taken, or the attitude about to be formed, a rational one? Is it consistent with the facts?

Rationality demands that the whole man become involved, that one acts as a total being. Irrationality, or insanity, is the action of a person based on only part of his being—only his emotions, or even the direct activity of the will apart from the mind or emotions. Rationality insists that the total man be involved; the mind must come into play.

The Deadly Power

At this point, therefore, Eve's mind is engaged. But a terrible thing has already happened to her. She does not realize it, but the arousing of her emotion, the strong desire to have this fruit that hangs there in all its tantalizing mystery, has already prepared her will to act. Even before her mind comes into play she wants the fruit and has secretly determined to have it.

Thus, when her mind comes into action it can no longer do so rationally. It cannot consider the facts as they are, but must act on the facts as they appear to her. Since it can no longer act rationally, it must rationalize. This is the deadly power of the mind. It has an amazing ability to rationalize, to twist the facts so they accord with desire, to satisfy the urge springing up within by justifying it, even though doing so must distort the facts.

Notice the process here. Eve looked at the fruit and said to herself, "It is good for food. It is something that will help me, something physically profitable. Never mind the long-range effects—I'm not interested in that—it will satisfy a present and immediate need, and what can be wrong with that?"

Second, she saw that it was "a delight to the eyes," which means it was pleasurable, it satisfied the aesthetic sense. This element is always present in temptation. Each of us is well aware (because we are all experts in it) that sin is fun—*for a while*! It has an element of pleasure about it and there is no use trying to pretend otherwise. It is the pleasure of sin which makes it so enticing and alluring. The desire to have that pleasure, at whatever cost, is really the essential element of temptation.

It feels good to indulge oneself. I love the feeling of splurging, of buying something that gives me pleasure. It feels great. That is why I do it, even though my mind may be telling me it will be ultimately harmful. It feels good to lose my temper. It feels good to hurt my wife when she has done something that angers me. Have you ever had the perverse delight of telling somebody off? Oh, how good that feels—for a while! It feels good even though you do not do it to someone's face but go out in the woods and scream at chipmunks. Even that relieves the pain for a bit.

There is pleasure in sin, and that is where its deceitfulness lies. As Eve saw the fruit she said, "It is good for food, and it is a delight to the eyes. It is beautiful to look at."

Finally, she saw that it was "to be desired to make one wise." In the book of James we have a reference to the wisdom in view here. Is something desired to make one wise? James reminds us there are two kinds of wisdom. There is the wisdom from above, from God; and there is a wisdom from below, which is "earthly, unspiritual, devilish" (James 3:15). Paul wrote to the Corinthians that "the wisdom of the world is folly with God" (1 Corinthians 3:19). But to us it appears alluring and satisfying.

John's first epistle describes a threefold appeal to the things the world values, corresponding to the appeal of the fruit to Eve's physical, sensual, and ego-satisfying desires:

> For all that is in the world, the lust of the flesh and the lust of the eyes and the pride of life, is not of the Father but is of the world (1 John 2:16).

The tree was "good for food." This corresponds to what John called "the lust of the flesh." The tree was also "a delight to the eyes." There is the "the lust of the eyes" John spoke of. Finally, the tree was "desired to make one wise." And that is John's "pride of life." So much of the philosophy of the world is based upon this "pride of life." We must discover ways of building ourselves up, enhancing self, taking special courses to develop the powers of our personality and charm and poise. All of this feeds the pride of life and satisfies the ego—but it is all the snare of the devil.

The Divine Order

Eve did not realize her mind had played a trick upon her. She had taken the apparent facts set before her by the enemy and had justified them, so that they looked reasonable, rational. The thing to do then, of course, was to give in. After all, anything that is good for food, pleasurable to the senses, and satisfying to the ego must be all right. But this is nothing less than a prostitution of the mind! It is reversing God's order.

In man as God made him, the order is to be: first, an appeal to the mind; then the stirring of the emotions based upon the facts presented to the mind; and then the two working together, the mind and emotions, to move the will.

This is why the gospel's appeal—this good news from God—always is addressed first to the mind throughout the Scriptures. The first appeal is never to the emotions but to the understanding. It is a presentation of certain historic facts which have significance, and the significance of those facts is what constitutes the good news. Paul says, "I preached to you the gospel . . . that Christ died for our sins"

(1 Corinthians 15:1,3). *He died* (the fact); *for our sins* (that is the significance of it); and *he rose again* to be a living Lord imparting himself to us.

This is the Good News, that Christ died to solve the problem of our rebellion and our estrangement from God, and he rose again to give us constantly his life, his grace, his strength. Upon these facts we can make a decision. These facts move us and stir us— they ought to, they are designed to. But there must come first the appeal to the mind. This is why any evangelism that does not begin with teaching is a false evangelism. Any evangelism that moves directly to an appeal to the will to act, or to the emotions to feel, is distorted and results in abortion rather than birth.

This technique of reversal prevails throughout the world. This is the technique of Madison Avenue and the advertising business. Thumb through a magazine and notice that all the advertisements are designed to arouse desire first. There sits a beautifully designed and painted sports car, displayed in living color. You cannot look at these beautiful advertisements without beginning to drool. There is a color TV set, the color so real it is startling. Then you look at your drab, black-and-white set in the corner, and you think, "How can I put up with a thing like that any longer?" Showrooms and store windows are designed to short-circuit the mind and appeal first to the will through the emotions.

This is the technique of politicians and propagandists. They too seek to arouse an emotional reaction first. They cleverly and carefully think through what will appeal to the emotions first and they start on that note. When the emotions are properly stirred, they present their plea for action, whatever the cause may be.

To arouse the middle class, the propagandists talk about *property values, free enterprise,* and *the American way of life.* To arouse blacks, the emotionally charged words might be *civil rights* or *apartheid.* By this sloganeering the propagandists attempt to arouse emotions first, realizing that when the mind comes into play (as it will), it will not think rationally but will rationalize; it will take facts and distort them to justify the desire that has been aroused.

This explains why efforts to convince people to stop cigarette smoking have been relatively ineffective. Cigarette smoking is not based upon rational observation. If it were, no one would smoke. Who wants lung cancer? But why do people smoke? Why do young men and women begin to smoke? I remember my own boyhood attempts at smoking, when I thought in some way it made me a man. In my desire to be grown up, smoking fed my sense of pride. The only way the effects of cigarette advertising can be counteracted is by fighting fire with fire—by arousing emotions in the opposite direction.

It would be entirely wrong to get the idea from this account that everything pleasurable is wrong, and everything right is boring, dull, and flat. This, of course, is what the enemy would like us to believe about God; anything God wants for us is dull, uninteresting, and lackluster, and only the exciting things are wrong.

When you begin to feel like this, remember that God designed our emotions. He made us to have feelings, and he intends to satisfy them. Desire is wrong, however, when it is contrary to the facts and thus prostitutes the mind, subjecting it to a rationalizing process, so that it must justify the facts. This is what is wrong.

Tempted Like Eve

We see this in the Lord Jesus Christ. He too went through a time of temptation. He experienced the same order of attack that Eve did—not in the garden this time, but in a wilderness, in a barren place removed from comfort, luxury, ease, and pleasantness. There in the barren wilderness, after forty days of fasting, he was tempted like Eve.

The first temptation came on the same level as it did to her. Just as she was tempted with food, so the tempter came to the Lord and said, "If you are the son of God, turn these stones into bread." But Jesus' answer was, "It is written, 'Man shall not live by bread alone.'" (Matthew 4:4). That is, bread is not the most important thing in life—God's will is. If you try to use bread for spiritual satisfaction, you are distorting God's design for man. That is not the purpose of bread. It is better to starve than to use bread for a purpose God did not intend. So Jesus used the facts of the situation—the way God made man—and rejected the enemy's appeal. He was saying, "It's not right, and I won't do it."

Then the enemy took him to a high mountain and showed him the kingdoms of the world in all their pomp, glory, and majesty. This dream has entranced men for centuries. Some have caught a vision of even part of the kingdoms of the world and have fallen in love with the glory of it. But Jesus was shown all the kingdoms of the world in their alluring glory, with the suggestion that if he would fall down and worship the enemy he could have all of it. This was clearly a delight to the eyes, something to titillate the senses and give a feeling of power. But our Lord rejected it because it did not accord with the facts: Man is made to worship God and God alone.

Then, you remember, the devil took him up to the temple and suggested he cast himself down to display his power. When the people saw he could do this without injury, they would acclaim him divine and he would gain popular appeal, the pride of life. But again he rejected it on the basis of the facts. He said, "No, it is written, 'You shall not tempt the Lord your God'" (Matthew 4:7). He was saying, "God is in charge of life, and I will not allow anything to enrich me but what comes through his hands." Thus he rejected the temptation.

At this point it is important to note that Eve had not yet sinned. Though her desire is aroused and her mind has justified it, still it would be possible for her to recover herself, though very difficult. But, as James tells us, desire when it conceives gives birth to sin. And at this point it is recorded that when she saw that it was desired to make one wise, "she took of its fruit and ate." She acted on a lie and thus fell into the sin of becoming her own god, of making up her own rules, in violation of her humanity.

Darkness Begins

But there was still hope for the race. Adam had not yet fallen, only Eve. It is not in Eve that the race fell; the responsibility lies with Adam. A battle has been lost, but not the war . . . yet. But then we read that after she took of the fruit and ate, "she also gave some to her husband, and he ate."

The ease with which Adam fell is dreadfully hard on the male ego. Think of it. Here is this whole account of the struggle of the tempter to reach Eve, and only one little line about Adam: "She gave to him, and he ate." Yet in those innocent but ominous words—"and he ate"—begins the darkness of a fallen humanity. The fatal twist now appears as mankind is transformed by this psychedelic drug (the forbidden fruit), and all men become the victim of a reverse psychology. Mastered by emotional urges, they are no longer rational beings.

What is the value of this account for us today? In this story we see that what Jesus says of the race is true: We are victims of a distortion that we are helpless to remedy. We cannot change our basic natures. No matter how desperately we try to be rational about things, we cannot see the facts rightly. We do not even see the whole range of facts, and ultimately we find ourselves the unconscious victims of emotional twisting.

If anything points up the absolute necessity for the new birth, it is this. Just as Jesus said, there is no other way out for humanity except through him. "I am the way, and the truth, and the life; no one comes to the Father, but by me" (John 14:6). There is no way to see reality apart from Jesus Christ. He opens my eyes, he restores balance to my life, and he redeems my humanity and makes it possible for me to distinguish between right and wrong.

How do we know what is right, among the welter of voices that call to us from every side, unless we judge them all by the voice of Jesus Christ? How can we find our way through the swamps of relativism that surround us, unless we are listening to the voice of the one who loved us and gave himself for us, that he might redeem us by destroying the works of the devil?

We must see once again, plainly and clearly, that there is no hope for us apart from the Lord Jesus. We must follow him, trusting his love, yielding ourselves to his redeeming grace.

6
THE
PACKAGE
DEAL

The evil act has finally been accomplished in the garden of Eden. "She took of its fruit and ate; and she also gave some to her husband, and he ate" (Genesis 3:6). When desire, conceived and rationalized, issues at last in its ultimate form, it becomes an act or a settled attitude of the heart.

Now we come to stage three in the process of temptation. James 1:15 describes it this way: "Sin when it is full-grown brings forth death." Remember that in the very beginning God had said to Adam and Eve concerning the forbidden fruit, "In the day that you eat of it you shall die" (Genesis 2:17). But the tempter had said to Eve, "You will not die." He openly and defiantly challenged God's pronouncement, saying, "Your eyes will be opened, and you will be like God . . . " (Genesis 3:5).

He made it sound glorious, exciting, and adventurous. He was implying to them, "When you eat of this fruit you need no longer depend on this old Lord of creation; you will be lords in your own right. You can make decisions like God does, and do what you want to do." This has been the subtle lie hanging over the whole human race from that day to this. But now the deed has been done, and we come to the moment of truth. Is the devil right? Or will they die?

> *Then the eyes of both were opened, and they knew that they were naked; and they sewed fig leaves together and made themselves aprons (3:7).*

At first the devil seems to be right. He said they would not die, and when they ate the fruit they did not drop dead. He said their eyes would be opened, and it is true that new knowledge was immediately theirs. They saw things they had not seen before. Does that mean that the devil was right? No, because from the moment they ate they began to die—exactly as God had said. In Romans, Paul writes, "Sin came into the world through one man and death through sin, and so death spread to all men" (Romans 5:12). The moment this occurred is the moment described in Genesis 3:7.

Signs of Death

In this passage we will discover the signs of death. Death is not simply the moment when breath leaves your body and you become a corpse. That is not death in its totality, but simply the end of death. It is the end of a process which has been going on for some time, the beginning of which was so subtle that perhaps you did not even recognize it. The *beginning* of death is traced in this Genesis account. The four things here which mark the beginning of death are found in every person in the world, without exception. These things plague the whole human race.

We all know that when we yield to temptation we experience pleasure. But what this account forces us to face is that with the pleasure comes something undesirable, a fallout from sin which we cannot escape. It is a package deal. If we choose to take the momentary pleasure, we cannot choose to evade its companion—death.

The first mark of death's beginning is this: "They knew that they were naked." They had been naked all along. God did not make Adam and Eve with clothes on, any more than he makes human beings with clothes on today. We come into this world naked. They too came into the world naked, but they did not know it until the Fall. Why not? Because they had never looked at themselves! Their interest was not toward themselves. They were self-less.

Before the Fall they were concerned about each other, and about the animals, and about the garden and the work assigned to them there. But now suddenly they saw themselves. This awareness of nakedness was the birth of self-consciousness. They saw themselves, and the immediate effect brought them shame and embarrassment.

Test this in your own life. Is this not your most serious trouble, the fact that you are conscious of yourself? Is this not where you struggle most? When we can forget ourselves, we do fine. We can speak, we can act, we can do many things well. But then the sense of self comes flooding over us, and we begin to fumble, to stammer, to blush. Suddenly we are all thumbs and left feet. Why? This is the effect of self-consciousness. But God did not make man that way. Man was never made to be conscious of himself. His interests were to lie outside himself; he was to be self-less.

Self-consciousness dogs every one of us every day, and the amazing thing is that to this very day we find that clothing helps us. Adam and Eve, when they discovered they were naked, immediately made rough clothing out of fig leaves. They made themselves aprons and covered themselves. This explains why we find it psychologically necessary to clothe ourselves. In mankind's fellowship with one another, clothing helps. It helps to make us feel more secure, more adequate, more able to face life. Like Adam and Eve, we find ourselves making clothes to cover our self-consciousness.

This is true at the psychological level as well. This is what lies behind the universal practice of creating an impression, of projecting an image, which is a form of psychological clothing. Physically, clothing is a way of changing our appearance so we look different than we actually are. So it is with projecting an image. It is a way of trying to get people to think we are different than we really are. This is why, at one time or another, we all find ourselves struggling with being honest, being open. We find it difficult to be so. We do not want people to see us or think of us as we are. So we avoid close contacts. We do not want to spend much time with any one-person because we are afraid he will see us as we are. You can see how this idea has permeated the race ever since the moment self-consciousness was born in an act of disobedience.

The Hiding Instinct

The second mark of disobedience is the tendency to hide:

And they heard the sound of the LORD God walking in the garden in the cool of the day, and the man and his wife hid themselves from the presence of the LORD God among the trees of the garden (3:8).

Hiding is an instinctive reaction to guilt, and reveals the fact of guilt. When one of my daughters was a baby she habitually sucked her thumb. When it carried over into late babyhood we tried to help her stop the habit. She began to feel very guilty about sucking her thumb. Often, when we would catch her doing so, she would take it out of her mouth and hide it under her dress. Now, who taught her to do that? No one. No one needs to teach us such things; these are instinctive reactions. She hid because she felt guilty.

Here, then, is the first description of a human conscience beginning to function, that inner torment we all recognize which cannot be turned off no matter how hard we try. In fact, often the harder we try to ignore it, the deeper it pierces and the more obdurate it becomes. Psychologists agree that guilt is universal. Without apparent reason or explanation, all of us, without exception, suffer from guilt. It haunts us, follows us, makes us afraid. We are afraid of the unknown, of the future, and of the unseen, just as Adam and Eve were.

But the LORD God called to the man, and said to him, "Where are you?" And he said, "I heard the sound of thee in the garden, and I was afraid, because I was naked; and I hid myself" (3:9-10).

That is the heritage of the Fall, this sense of guilt. It is death at work. But there is still a third aspect of this death:

He said, "Who told you that you were naked? Have you eaten of the tree of which I commanded

you not to eat?" The·man said, "The woman
whom thou gavest to be with me, she gave me fruit
of the tree, and I ate." Then the LORD God said
to the woman, "What is this that you have
done?" The woman said, "The serpent beguiled
me, and I ate" (3:11-13).

Here is the oldest game in the world, the favorite
indoor sport of the whole race—passing the buck.
The Lord said to them, "What is this that you have
done?" And Adam said, "Well, the woman that you
gave to me, *she* gave me the fruit, and I ate. It's her
fault." The woman said, "Well, it's not my fault, it's
the serpent's fault. The serpent beguiled me, and I
ate."

Who Do You Blame?

This is the first human attempt to deal with guilt.
It is exactly the same way in which we try to relieve
guilt. See how these factors are all related. It is self-
consciousness which is the basic, fundamental
wrongness about human life. This is what produces
guilt. Our awareness of self makes us ashamed,
embarrassed, and guilty. Then, in order to evade this
sense of guilt, we do what Adam did. We say, "Well,
it's not my fault. I'm but a victim of circumstance."
He took it, you see, like a man; he blamed it on his
wife. And she passed it along to the serpent.

But behind both excuses is the unspoken suggestion, very clear in this account, *that it is really God's*
fault. "The woman whom *thou* gavest me . . . " says
Adam. "If you had never given me this woman I
would never have fallen into this sin." The woman
immediately passes it on: "It is because you allowed
the serpent to come into this garden, that's the
trouble." Both point the finger ultimately at God:
"It's all your fault."

This attitude pervades society and the whole of history. It is what married couples say to one another all the time. The biggest problem in solving the tangles of a marriage relationship is to get the two to stop blaming each other. That is the hardest thing to do. But if they do it, the battle is two-thirds won.

This is also the primary cause of racial strife. Each race is pointing a finger at the other and saying, "It's your fault!" This is what nations do on the international scene. We find ourselves universally yielding to this tendency to blame another and thus, ultimately, to blame God. Of course, we do not say it that way. Very seldom do you find someone coming out openly, outrightly, and blatantly saying, "It's God's fault!" But that is what lies beneath the surface; we are blaming God for the whole thing, trying to turn guilt into fate and to make of ourselves mere innocent victims, suffering from a breakdown in creation for which God is responsible.

The fourth result this account reveals is found in verse 16:

> *To the woman he said, "I will greatly multiply your pain in childbearing; in pain you shall bring forth children."*

And in verse 19, God says to Adam,

> *In the sweat of your face you shall eat bread till you return to the ground, for out of it you were taken; you are dust, and to dust you shall return.*

Pain, sweat, and death. Here are the limits of life. These are the prison walls that hem us in and mock all our hunger and yearning after freedom and fullness. Is it not clear that the whole race suffers from a sense of loss, a sense of limitation? Each one of us knows the feeling. We know there is more to life than we are experiencing—and how we crave it! How we long to find it somehow, somewhere.

We pore over travel brochures. We read about new opportunities for work. We join a club, or seek new relationships. We adopt a hobby. We desperately try to find some way to enter into the fullness we feel life ought to offer. We know it is there, but we have lost the way to it. Every effort we make, every step we take, every channel we follow, finds us flung back by these three things: pain; hard, grinding toil; and the black wall of death.

Why is it that we all have a sense of urgency about our work? Why are we forever saying, "Let's make the years count, let's use time to the full"? Why do we use calendars and clocks? It is because we realize we must die. Our time is limited. We are surrounded by walls we cannot break through. Every effort we make, if pressed too far, results in pain, struggle, and death.

This is what happened to Adam and Eve. Their eyes were indeed opened, but this is what they saw: the hard, cruel facts of life lived apart from dependence on God. They immediately knew a sense of self-consciousness, an awareness of guilt, an urge to blame the other, and that terrible, empty, hollow feeling of limitation, a sense of loss. What a cruel and dreary world these factors have produced. They are what the Bible calls "the works of the devil," works which he is free to accomplish because man has given him opportunity in the disobedient act of his heart.

The Second Adam

But we cannot leave the story there. We must remember that if there was a first Adam, from whose misdeed we all suffer, the good news is that there is also a second Adam, a man who came to reverse the works of the devil, to free us, to loose us from their evil control. What does Jesus Christ do about these things?

What does he do about my self-consciousness? What does he do about my sense of having to depend upon myself? How does he handle the guilt, embarrassment, and sense of inadequacy that immediately flood me when I realize I don't have what it takes to meet the demands of life? What does he do?

He turns my eyes from myself to himself. I learn to say with Paul, "I have been crucified with Christ; it is no longer I . . . but Christ" (Galatians 2:20). He lives in me and whatever I do is done not out of dependence on myself, but it is Jesus at work in me—and he is the adequate one. As soon as I believe and act upon this, I lose my self-consciousness. I become self-less. My life begins to manifest the outgoing givingness of the self-less Christ.

Such is the nature of the life you live in Christ. He destroys the tormenting self-consciousness that creates the embarrassment of life.

What, then, does he do about my guilt? Ah, here is a glorious word! He comes to me when I stumble, when I fail or falter, when I find myself doing what I don't want to and loathing myself because of it, and he says to me, "If any man be in Christ *there is no condemnation*. You don't need to worry; I know you do these things. I know you have given way, and that you will give way. I know you don't easily choose good and repudiate evil. I know this—but I love you and have died in your place. If you will look at this wrong thing and simply regard it honestly, as it is, immediately there is no condemnation. You are as loved as you ever were, you are as much mine as you ever were. Don't look back at the past; start right here with me, right now, and let's go on."

How does this affect my urge to blame another person? Jesus helps me greatly at this point. He says to me, "Look, I'll give you the formula by which you can work out the problems of your life with other people. First, remove the beam that is in your own eye, then you'll see clearly how to help someone else." When I see what someone else is doing wrong but I don't know how to help him stop it, then I know I am failing to first remove the beam in my own eye. I'm not following Jesus' directions.

But if I *will* follow him; if I stop and say, "What am *I* doing that makes him (or her) act this way to me?" then the situation wonderfully changes and I find that everyone begins to act differently to me; the whole world is different. The problem was not with others; it was with me. This is what Jesus helps me see. Openly, honestly, forthrightly, he tells me where the problem is.

What does he do about my fear of pain and sweat and death? You know what he does, don't you? He does not remove you from these things. In fact, you will often find yourself more frequently in them as a believer than perhaps you were before. The pain is still there, the need for toil is still there. And I know—and you know—that a time will come when we must face the fact of death. None of us can carry on our work forever. Each of us must come to the place where we fold our hands, and our spirit leaves this body, and we are dead. What does Jesus do about this?

The Doorway

He goes with me into each dreaded circumstance, and I discover that what was to me a grievous cross, where something within me is put to death and which I fear, becomes a doorway into a new and greater experience than I could ever have dreamed. It is the old story of the cross and the resurrection. You can never experience the resurrection glory unless you have first experienced the death of a cross. Pain is transmuted into something different, a quiet peace which, though the pain is still there, makes it all worthwhile.

Like you, I look back on the painful experiences of my life and say, "Those were the hours I learned my greatest lessons. Those were the times when God spoke to me as at no other time." Thank God for them. Then look at life's demands for labor, sweat, and toil, and know that these are also the moments when we find ourselves the happiest, moments that produce the greatest gladness, peace, and joy. And at last, when we cross the river of death, it is only an incident.

I know it will be so. It is but an incident, a momentary flash, and then all the greatness of God's glorious promise will begin to unfold in its shining reality. "O death, where is thy victory? O death, where is thy sting?" (1 Corinthians 15:55).

This is why Jesus Christ came. He finds us as people, human beings, involved in the nitty-gritty, hurly-burly of life, the struggle, the heartache, the grief, the sweat, blood, and tears, and he transmutes those things into patience and peace and joy. Christianity is not something to be experienced only in a religious service on Sunday—that's merely the whipped cream on top. The wonderful body of Christianity is mingled with the flow and flood of life itself. This is what makes it all so glorious. Jesus reverses the devil's activity, and releases us from the devil's works.

What happens when, as Christians, we choose the wrong? We die. This is inevitable. "To set the mind on the flesh is death," Paul tells us (Romans 8:6). If we deliberately choose to disobey our Lord we will experience the fourfold death that follows inevitably in the great package deal of life. It is the law of inevitable consequences which Paul describes so clearly when he says, "Whatever a man sows, that he will also reap" (Galatians 6:7). But the glory of the gospel is that the other side is true as well. "He who sows to the Spirit will from the Spirit reap eternal life" (6:8). Sow to the Spirit and you reap life—life as you have never known it before.

If you sow to the Spirit, if you obey and walk in fellowship with the Son of God, then in this life you will see the sure reversing of all these evil things we have been looking at—and in their place will be the fellowship, the joy, the glory, and the riches that are in Jesus Christ.

May God help us to cease our disobedience, to stop challenging the authority of God's word, to flee our apathetic lethargy that refuses to venture on the facts that Jesus Christ reveals to us.

And let us begin right now.

7
GOD AT WORK

Once again let us study Genesis 3—but this time looking not at man but at God.

For centuries a dirty lie about God has been making the rounds. This lie says that at man's fall, God ruthlessly lowered the boom, that he gave guilty Adam and Eve no chance to explain but simply tracked them down, sternly rebuked them (my children would say he yelled at them), began cursing everything in sight, and ended by booting the couple out of the garden, slamming and locking the door behind them.

Nothing could be further from the truth! We must trace very carefully God's actions in this account, because this is the same way God will treat us after we fall into wrongdoing.

God begins his dealings with man by raising three questions. The first is found in verses 8 and 9:

> And they heard the sound of the LORD God walking in the garden in the cool of the day, and the man and his wife hid themselves from the presence of the LORD God among the trees of the garden. But the LORD God called to the man, and said to him, "Where are you?"

All religions, apart from Christianity, begin with man seeking after God. Only the Bible starts with God seeking after man. This highlights an essential difference between our Christian faith and the world's religions. Furthermore, this question is matched by the first question recorded in the New Testament. Here God asks Adam, "Where are you?" while the first question asked in Matthew comes from certain wise men who ask, "Where is he?"

If we take this account in the garden literally (as I believe we must), then it is clear that God habitually appeared to Adam in some visible form; for now Adam and Eve in their guilt and awareness of nakedness hide from God when they hear his footsteps in the garden. This indicates a customary action on God's part. He came in the cool of the day, not because that was more pleasant for him, but because it was more pleasant for man.

We know from Scripture that whenever God appears visibly it is always the second Person of the Godhead, the Son. If that is true, then we have here what is called a *theophany*, that is, a visible manifestation of God before the incarnation. Thus the one here who asks of Adam and Eve, "Where are you?" is the same one of whom men later would ask, "Where is he who was born King of the Jews?"

Notice the importance of this question, "Where are you?" Suppose you were on your way to a friend's house, but got lost and called him up to direct you. His first question would have to be "Where are you?" He would have to know where you are to have a starting point for his directions.

Today we are seeking a way out of the confusing situation prevailing in our world. We will never do it until we start with this question God first asked man—"Where are you?"

Where am I? Perhaps many are unable to be helped today because they cannot or will not answer that question. Ask it of yourself now: Where are you? In the course of your life, from birth to death, growing (as you hope you are growing) in stability of character, trustworthiness, integrity, all these qualities we admire in others and want in ourselves—where are you? How far have you come? Until you can answer that, in some sense at least, there is no possibility of helping you. What do you say?

Perhaps you will have to say, "I don't know where I am. I only know I am not where I ought to be, nor where I want to be. That's all I can say." If that is all you can say, at least it's an honest answer and therefore the most helpful answer you can give.

God's second question is even more significant:

And he [Adam] said, "I heard the sound of thee in the garden, and I was afraid, because I was naked; and I hid myself." He [God] said, "Who told you that you were naked?" (Genesis 3:10).

Let us be sure we read this question rightly. God is not asking Adam, "Look, who let the cat out of the bag about this? What rascal has been telling you tales out of school?" No, this is a rhetorical question. God does not expect a direct answer; it is a question designed to make Adam think.

An Inner Change

God is asking, "How do you know this? You say you're naked; you didn't know that before. From what source has this knowledge come? Something has happened, a change has occurred; where did your knowledge come from?" The answer, of course, is that no one told him. Then how did he know?

It did not come from without at all, but from within. A change had occurred within him, and instinctively he sensed that change and knew something he did not know before. An evil knowledge had come to Adam, just as God said it would. The tree of which he partook was the tree of "the knowledge of good and evil," and by partaking he immediately gained an evil knowledge. From where did it come? From within. It was the birth of conscience, that strange faculty within that tells us often what we do not want to hear. This is what God awakens Adam to see.

To sense the full significance of this, we must link it with the first question, "Where are you?" which had only one proper answer: "I'm not where I want to be. I'm lost, hopelessly lost, hidden. I don't know where I am." And why don't we know? Why is it that we have such trouble pinpointing ourselves in our progress and relationship to the world around us? It is because of something within, isn't it? Remember what Jesus said—

"There is nothing outside a man which by going into him can defile him. . . . What comes out of

a man is what defiles a man. For from within,
out of the heart of man, come evil thoughts, forni-
cation, theft, murder, adultery, coveting, wicked-
ness, deceit, licentiousness, envy, slander, pride,
foolishness. All these evil things come from
within, and they defile a man" (Mark 7:15-
23).

It is what I am within that makes me ashamed and guilty, and sends me scrambling for fig leaves to cover myself up. Someone has well said, "If the best of men had his innermost thoughts written on his forehead, he'd never take his hat off." We know this is true. The basic, fundamental issue of humanity is not what is happening outside, but what is happening within us.

Now God moves to his third question. It is in two parts, one addressed to the man and one to the woman.

"Have you eaten of the tree of which I commanded
you not to eat?" The man said, "The woman
whom thou gavest to be with me, she gave me fruit
of the tree, and I ate." Then the LORD God said
to the woman, "What is this that you have
done?" The woman said, "The serpent beguiled
me, and I ate" (Genesis 3:11-13).

There is something very interesting here. God asks them both the same question. He is saying to each, "Tell me, what is it you did? Specifically, definitely, clearly—what is it?" But there is an exquisite touch of delicacy and grace here which I hope you do not miss. He does not put the question in the same form to each. To the man he is forthright and blunt. "Have you eaten of the tree of which I commanded you not to eat?" But to the woman he puts the question much more softly and gently. It is comforting to me to realize how fully God understands women and to see him put the question to her so gently. He says, "Tell me in your own way now, what is this that you have done?"

In their answer it is significant that both come out at the same place. Each blames someone else (a response we call "human nature," since it is so universal), but when they come to their final statement they both use exactly the same words, "and I ate."

Reduced to the Facts

This is where God wants to bring them. This is what the Bible calls "repentance." It is a candid statement of the facts with no attempt to evade, color, or clothe them in any way. It is a simple, factual statement to which they are both reduced: "and I ate." This is the point to which God has sought to lead them.

Do you see how these questions have followed a certain course? God has made them say, first, "We're not where we ought to be—we know that. We ought not to be lost. We ought not to require a question like this, 'Where are you?'" Then God has made them see that they are lost because something has happened within them. They are *where* they are because of *what* they are, and it all happened because they sinned, they disobeyed, they ate the forbidden food. God has led them gently, graciously, and yet unerringly to the place where each of them, in his own way, has said, "Yes, Lord, I sinned; I ate."

This is as far as man can ever go in correcting evil. He can do no more. But this immediately provides the ground for God to act. This is where he constantly seeks to bring us. This is seen throughout the whole Bible, in Old and New Testaments alike. When God is dealing with men he seeks to bring them to the place where they acknowledge what is wrong.

Remember Jesus' dealing with the woman of Samaria at the well? After they discoursed about the meaning of the water, he awakened her curiosity and interest by offering her living water so she would not have to come to the well to draw. He then forthrightly gave the command, "Go and call your husband."

This elicits the only answer the woman could honestly give. "I have no husband," she says. Then Jesus lays it out right before her. "That's true," he says, "you have no husband. You have had five husbands, and the man you are living with now is not your husband; in this you said truly." He commends her for speaking the truth. From that point on he moves to open her eyes to the character of the one standing before her (John 4:7-26).

This is exactly what God wants to do with us. He finds us in our failure, our estrangement, our guilt, our sense of nakedness and loss, and immediately he moves to bring us to repentance. We misunderstand his moving. We think he is dragging us before some tribunal to chastise or punish us, but he is not. He is simply trying to get us to face the facts. This is what he does here with Adam and Eve. As John says, "If we confess our sins, he is faithful and just, and will forgive our sins and cleanse us from all unrighteousness" (1 John 1:9).

As soon as Adam and Eve say these telling words, "and I ate," there are no more questions from God. There is no more prodding or probing. God now speaks to the serpent, to the woman, and to the man. What he says to the man and the woman is not punishment, as we will see shortly, but grace. How badly we have misread these passages in Genesis! And when he gets through, we read these wonderful words:

> *And the* LORD *God made for Adam and for his wife garments of skins, and clothed them (Genesis 3:21).*

Here is the apparent beginning of animal sacrifices: To make animal-skin garments for Adam and Eve, God must have shed blood, sacrificing the animals to clothe Adam and Eve. This would be but a picture, as all animal sacrifices are but pictures—a kind of kindergarten of grace—to teach the great truth that God eternally declares to men and women. Ultimately it is God himself who bears the pain, the hurt, the agony of our sins. As John the Baptist said, "Behold, the Lamb of God, who takes away the sin of the world!" (John 1:29).

Orphan Lambs

Paul uses a wonderful phrase in Ephesians, "accepted in the beloved" (Ephesians 1:6 KJV). When we have acknowledged our guilt, when we have acknowledged that what we have done is contrary to what God wants, and we stand before him without trying to defend ourselves, then, Paul says, we are "accepted in the beloved."

There were many sheep farms in the area of Montana where I grew up. Spring was the season when little lambs were born. But spring in Montana can be brutal; sleet storms can come whirling down out of the north, and snow can still be three or four feet deep on the prairies. Often there are long periods of bitter cold during lambing season.

In that kind of weather, many of the lambs and ewes die. As a result, sheep farmers have many mothers whose newborn lambs have died, and many newborn lambs whose mothers have died. A simple way to solve the problem, it would seem, would be to take the lambs without mothers and give them to the mothers without lambs. But with sheep it is not that simple. If you take a little orphan lamb and put it in with a mother ewe, the mother will immediately go to it and sniff it all over, but then shake her head as though to say, "Well, that's not our family odor." She will butt the lamb away, refusing to have anything to do with it.

But sheep ranchers have devised a means of solving this problem. They take the mother's own little dead lamb, skin it, take the skin and tie it onto the orphan lamb. Then they put the little lamb with this ungainly skin flopping around—eight legs, two heads—in with the mother. She pays no attention at all to the way it looks, but she sniffs it all over again, and then she nods her head, all is well, and the lamb is allowed to nurse. What has happened? The orphan lamb has been accepted in the beloved one.

There came a time when God's Lamb lay dead on our behalf and God took us orphans—he does it all the time—and clothed us in his righteousness, his acceptability, his dearness and nearness to him. Thus we stand "accepted in the beloved," received in his place. This is where repentance brings us.

It Doesn't End Here

But repentance is not only for the beginning of the Christian life. It is the way you start as a Christian, true. You come to God, like Adam and Eve, and say, "Yes, Lord, I'm the one. I've been running from you, I've been hiding from you, I've been estranged from you. It's because of what I've done. No one else is to blame but me." Then immediately God says, "I've

taken care of all that. My Lamb has died for you and
you stand in his place, acceptable to me." This is the
way you begin the Christian life.

But it is only the beginning. Repentance is the
basis on which the whole Christian life is built. We
must be continually repenting when we fail or fall
back on a way of living God has said is not right. I
find that I am repenting far more than I ever did before, about things I never dreamed of repenting of before, because I am learning more and more that the
Christian life is lived on a totally different basis.

I must repent of my self-dependence, and so must
you. "Without me," says the Lord Jesus, "you can do
nothing." If you try to do anything apart from dependence on him and his work through you, you need
to repent, to change your mind, to accept again the
covering of God, the clothing of his grace, the cleans-
ing of his love.

This may, perhaps, occur dozens of times a day
until we learn at last, little by little, to walk in this
way and to count on his working. He is ours, and all
that he is belongs to us. This is standard operating
procedure, not just emergency treatment.

Now that Adam and Eve are standing before God,
having acknowledged their sin—having said the
same thing about it that God said, having admitted
that they did the thing God said was wrong—his
whole relationship to them changes. He is on their
side, he is "for" them, as Paul tells us God is "for" us
in Romans 8:31. Of course, he had been this way all
along, but Adam and Eve could not enjoy it until
they repented.

Neither can we.

8
THE
DEVIL'S BURDEN

When Adam and Eve acknowledged their guilt, God immediately became their defender. His first word is to the tempter, and it is one of scorching judgment.

This is exactly in line with the promise given in 1 John 2:1—"But if any one does sin, we have an advocate [a defender] with the Father, Jesus Christ the righteous." As long as we defend ourselves, he cannot defend us; but when we are ready to stop defending ourselves, the Lord becomes our wholly adequate defender.

This same glorious defense is here in this scene; the Friend of sinners stood in Eden on that faraway day.

Hear him speak to the devil:

The LORD God said to the serpent, "Because you have done this, cursed are you above all cattle, and above all wild animals; upon your belly you shall go, and dust you shall eat all the days of your life" (Genesis 3:14).

These words addressed to the tempter are not a reference to the fact that snakes go around on their bellies. True, they do that, but they do not literally eat dust, as the word here says. This is figurative language—the words depict and describe humiliation and utter degradation. To this day one of the most humiliating things that anyone can be forced to do is to lie on his belly in the dirt. It means pride has been brought low; he is humiliated, shamed. "To eat dirt" has entered the language as an expression of humiliation.

Curse of Humiliation

These are significant words. Many Bible scholars believe a passage in Isaiah describes the fall of the devil. He is called there Lucifer, the Day Star, Son of the Morning, the angel who was created first among all the angels of heaven. In the pride of his heart he began to say to himself, "I will be like the Most High, I will act like God" (see Isaiah 14:12-20). He is clearly identifiable with the tempter in the garden, for he suggests this same thing to Eve. "If you eat of this fruit," he says, "you will be like the Most high, you will be like God, knowing good and evil."

As far as we can judge, the fall of Satan occurred a long time before this scene in the garden of Eden. But it seems almost certain that when Satan fell he was immediately transformed into a being of malevolent hatred against God. Perhaps there was a time when repentance was possible, but it is likely that at this period in history the devil had passed beyond that stage. Yet judgment had not yet been carried out upon him.

The significant thing here is the divine announcement to the devil of his ultimate judgment. Here he learns, perhaps for the first time, that his judgment would occur on this planet—that here, where he had so successfully derailed humanity through its first parents, he was to be put under an eternal curse. He was to suffer continual humiliation and repeated failure.

The next time you watch an old western and you hear the hero say, "All right, you snake, crawl out on yore belly!" or perhaps, "Jest give me a chance and I'll make him lick the dust!" remember that you're watching a Sunday school lesson in action! Perhaps this incident may help us understand why westerns are so popular, though they always have the same plot, the same basic characters, and invariably the same ending. They dramatize the eternal battle of the ages, the unconscious struggle that goes on in each of us. We want the "good guys" to win because we believe what God has said here—that it is the devil's due to end up always in humiliation and defeat.

"Well," you say, "that may be true in westerns, but not in life. In life it's not the good guys that win, but the evil ones." Ruthless power seems to always triumph over good, while the good end up as victims of senseless tragedy. What about those six million Jews who died under Hitler? What about the blacks, Mexicans, and many others who have been persecuted, hounded, smashed and killed, in so many places in our world? What about the looting and burning of villages in Vietnam, Cambodia, and Afghanistan? Is this an example of the devil's ultimate humiliation? What about the rape and murder of women and children in so many hell-spots of the world? You say, "All this is evidence that the devil's defeat is but a fairy tale. It occurs in fiction, but it doesn't work out in fact."

Yet Genesis 3 declares that it *does* occur in fact, it is *true*. The devil will always end up as the defeated one, the humiliated one, fallen on his belly in the dust, eating dirt. The problem is, we don't wait until the end of the story. We wait when it's on television because it only lasts a half-hour; but life we turn off before it gets through.

Keep looking, however, and see how this account tells us exactly how God proposes to accomplish the devil's humiliation.

> *I will put enmity between you and the woman,*
> *and between your seed and her seed; he shall*
> *bruise your head, and you shall bruise his heel*
> *(Genesis 3:15).*

This is surely one of the most remarkable verses in the Bible. It was called by the early church fathers "the Protoevangelium," which means the first preaching of the gospel. It is a clear promise and the first mention in the Bible of a coming Redeemer.

Several unusual features about this remarkable verse reveal the divine hand. First, it predicts an unending enmity between two classes of humanity. Here begins the two divisions of humanity into which the Bible consistently divides the race. First there is enmity between Eve and the serpent, between the tempter and the woman. "I will put enmity between you and the woman," says God. This is certainly understandable. We can see why Eve would detest this one who had betrayed her by his lies, and as the effects of the Fall would become more and more evident in her life, she would feel a continuing abhorrence toward this one who had so cleverly and ruthlessly led her astray.

On the other hand, the enemy would surely hate her because she was now the object of God's love, and God's hand of protection was around her. But it was not enmity between the woman and the devil alone, but between his seed and her's—that is, between the devil's seed and the woman's seed.

Seed of a Woman

This startling prophecy finds fulfillment in the virgin birth of Jesus. Some tell us today the virgin birth is an unimportant doctrine, but it is really one of the most essential doctrines concerning our Lord.

This concept of the seed of the woman is unique. Nowhere else in the Bible is there such an expression. Everywhere else descent in Scripture is reckoned through the male line. It is the seed of the man that determines the line of descent, and all the genealogies of the Bible trace ancestry through the male. The father's name is given, and when the mother's name is given it is only incidental, referring to the wife of so-and-so.

Most societies continue this today. Most families bear the man's name. When a couple gets married normally the woman drops her name and takes her husband's name. The name of the ensuing family bears the man's name; it is the male's seed which is the line of descent. But here we are distinctly told that the one who is to bruise the serpent's head is the seed of the woman. Now in all of history there is only one who can fulfill that condition, Jesus of Nazareth.

Matthew's Gospel tells us that when Joseph found Mary was pregnant, even before they had come together—honest man that he was, gentle man that he

was—"he determined to put her aside privately."
This was the kindest thing he could do, the most gra-
cious way he could handle the situation, because he
knew the child was not his. But an angel appeared
and told him, "That which is conceived in her is of
the Holy Spirit" (Matthew 1:20). Luke refers to the
virgin birth as well. Thus in the Gospels it is firmly
established that Jesus was born of a virgin—of a
woman but not of a man. He was the seed of a
woman.

So the seed is Christ. This impressive prophecy
looks across the centuries to the day when Jesus
would be born of Mary in Bethlehem. This is con-
firmed by the masculine pronoun which follows the
statement, "I will put enmity between you and the
woman, and between your seed and her seed; *he* shall
bruise your head. . . ." The fulfillment of this promise, the seed of the woman, would be a man, born
only of a woman.

God's word to the serpent continues, ". . . and you
shall bruise his heel." Old Testament believers could
not see what was involved in this, but now we know
it meant the humble birth at Bethlehem, the silent
years in Nazareth, the opposition and hatred at Jerusalem, the darkness of Gethsemane, the blood and
death of Golgotha—all this was the bruising of the
heel. Then there came the bruising of the serpent's
head in the glory of the resurrection morning. This
whole promise is clearly fulfilled in Jesus Christ.

Brother Abel

But it is not *only* Christ, for now we know that "the
seed" was not only an individual, but a people,
against whom the enmity of Satan would continue
throughout the age, for the whole history of the race.
Thus the seed is not only Jesus but all who are "in

Christ," both Old and New Testament believers. The division here between two classes is not along racial or physical lines (there is no physical paternity of the devil), but along spiritual and moral lines.

In the next chapter we learn that Cain was the first of "the seed of the devil"; but the Pharisees of Jesus' day were Cain's brothers, and Jesus said to them, "You are of your father the devil, and your will is to do your father's desires" (John 8:44). The Pharisees of our own day belong to the same classification. On the other hand, Abel, Cain's brother in the flesh, was the first of "the seed of the woman," redeemed humanity. All who trust in Jesus Christ today are brothers and sisters of Abel, members of that divine family who have, by faith, become part of the seed which is Christ.

Paul undoubtedly refers to this verse when he says to the Christians in Rome,

> *For while your obedience is known to all, so that I rejoice over you, I would have you wise as to what is good and guileless to what what is evil; then the God of peace will soon crush Satan under your feet (Romans 16:19-20).*

There, you see, is the bruising of the serpent's head, to be accomplished not only by Christ, but also for those who are "in Christ." Again Paul probably refers to this passage when he writes in 2 Timothy 1:9 that God

> *saved us and called us with a holy calling, not in virtue of our works but in virtue of his own purpose and the grace which he gave us in Christ Jesus ages ago.*

The phrase "ages ago" is literally "before the age-times." Here he refers to a promise of life God gave which would come through an individual, and which was given before men began to count time. This may well refer to this promise in the garden of Eden of a coming Redeemer who would be the seed of the woman and the source of life. Paul uses a similar phrase in Titus 1:2, where he speaks of the "hope of eternal life which God, who never lies, *promised before the age-times.*"

The situation is clear: All those who have come into this race through the normal line of descent from Adam, as the seed of Adam, were born into the devil's control. But God is calling out a seed of promise. All who exercise faith in this Promised One, whether it be faith before he came or faith in him now, are "in Christ" and are also the seed of the woman. Between these two (the devil's seed and the woman's seed) is enmity—unending enmity.

Surely we, who know Jesus Christ, experience this enmity frequently. Scripture describes it as the flesh warring against the spirit—and who of us has not felt it? Perhaps even now you are sensing this unending struggle. We know what God wants of us, we are learning how to walk in the Spirit, and yet often we desire to walk in the flesh—and we do. Because of this unending enmity between these two, we are constantly exposed to attack and temptation.

The enmity extends to individuals as well. Galatians speaks of those born of the flesh who persecute "the children of promise" (Galatians 4:28-29). How the world hates the truth of God, and seeks to ridicule it and stamp it out! The world bans the Bible and burns the saints.

Strange Twist of God

But then a remarkable thing happens—this is the great thrust of the passage. The devil's burden is that his very victories become also his defeats. There is this strange twist by which God in his power and wisdom turns the devil's victories into utter defeat. He succeeds in bruising Christ's heel, but that bruised heel is what finally crushes the serpent's head. You can see this in the cross. It was the bruising on the cross that made possible the smashing triumph of the resurrection. You can see it also in the events of your own life and in the events of world history.

Consider the deaths of those six million Jews under Hitler. We can hardly contemplate such a hideous thing. Yet it was that event, ghastly as it was, that made possible the birth of the nation Israel, setting the stage for the fulfillment of scriptural promises going unanswered for centuries. The enemy's attempt to stamp out God's people—this strange nation marked out by God as peculiarly his own among the nations—was turned into defeat and is now used to establish them in the land of promise.

In a remarkable way, the distortion of truth in the stupid rituals and empty ceremonies of the medieval church in Martin Luther's day prepared the hearts of Europe for the blazing glory of the Reformation. People were so revolted by what they were seeing, their hearts were so empty, they were so fed up with materialistic indulgences and external approaches to God, that they cried out in desperation for a note of reality. When Martin Luther nailed the ninety-five theses to the door of the church at Wittenberg, he struck a spark that caught fire throughout the tinder of Europe—tinder prepared by the devil. It was the devil's efforts that made possible the blazing fires of the Reformation.

We look back thirty or forty years and long for the days when youth were content with getting an education, finding a job, making money, going to church every Sunday, and fulfilling the moral demands of life. We think, "Oh, those were the good old days—before youth got so wild and rebellious and uncontrollable." But we are blind to the frequent hypocrisy of those days, to the empty materialism, to the blurring of human values that was so common and so widely accepted.

The devil has used this rebelliousness to push youth into revolt; but that is not the whole story. The glorious fact is that because of their rebellion there is a growing spirit of honest searching after truth that will not be denied. Young people are fed up with superficial answers, and they will have nothing to do with the shallow, empty, materialistic gas they have been fed by a previous generation. They are looking desperately for reality.

Surely this is the greatest hour in our nation's history for young people to learn about Jesus Christ. I remember those dark days of the Depression when the Christian cause was scorned in intellectual circles. You could hardly bear a Christian witness on campus without being labeled a militant fundamentalist and alienating everyone. But now the campuses are wide open to hear what Jesus Christ is saying. There has never been such a moment. And who set it up? The devil did!

I always rejoice at reading in Philippians of Paul's imprisonment. I laugh with joy at God's skill in turning this situation to his own glory. Paul says, "What has happened to me has really served to advance the gospel" (Philippians 1:12). And what had happened? God had chosen Nero, the most wicked and monstrous emperor the Roman Empire ever knew, and appointed him to head the Committee for the Evangelization of the Roman Empire! He set him to the task of searching the empire for the finest young men of the land and bringing them to Rome. Then, every so often, he was to pick out one of the best of these and chain him to the apostle Paul for six hours. You can predict what the result would be. One by one these young men were coming to Christ—the finest young men of Rome. It is undoubtedly from this band that many of the young men came whose names are recorded in the New Testament. When Paul closes his letter to the Philippians he says, "All the saints greet you, *especially those of Caesar's household*" (Philippians 4:22).

Today as well, God is turning the tables on the devil. Satan overreaches himself today just as he always has. It is his fate to end up as the villain in the old western melodramas: Having trapped his victims and thinking he's on the verge of success, he suddenly is foiled when the hero arrives and saves the day.

The same principle operates in our own lives. Which of us has not had an experience similar to Paul's, when that nagging, wretched thorn in the flesh prodded and probed him? How he hated it, and asked God to take it away. But God said, "No, I won't. My grace is sufficient for you." As Paul pondered this he realized what God meant, and he writes it down for us. He says, "I see now that it was given to me by God. It was the 'messenger of Satan,' true; yet God allowed it to come and permitted it to remain so I might be kept from becoming proud, and thus no longer be useful to God. It is this that humiliates me, humbles me, and makes me depend upon God and not myself. Therefore," he says, "I will glory in my infirmities, for out of weakness I am made strong" (see 2 Corinthians 12:7-10).

This is the devil's burden. Do you know anything more encouraging than that? The God we serve is continually taking the worst the devil can do and turning it into glorious victory. You will find that principle running through the Bible, from Genesis to Revelation. This is Christianity, entirely different from the principles by which the world seeks to work out its problems. Perhaps it has been best expressed in the words of the poet James Russell Lowell.

> *Though the cause of evil prosper*
> *yet 'tis truth alone is strong.*
> *Truth forever on the scaffold,*
> *Wrong forever on the throne—*

It does appear that way, doesn't it? It looks as though truth is pinned down and crucified, and wrong sits forever on the throne. Evil seems to rule, walking unhampered across the lives of millions. Yet the poet is right—it is not the throne of evil that ultimately succeeds; it is the cross, the place of apparent despair and defeat, the place of poverty, emptiness, and nothingness.

> *Yet that scaffold sways the future,*
> *and behind the dim unknown*
> *Standeth God within the shadows,*
> *keeping watch above his own.*

This is the devil's burden. Be glad you're not on his side—or are you?

9
LOVE'S DISCIPLINES

Pain, toil, subjection, and sorrow are the inevitable consequences of human disobedience to God. They were in the beginning, and they still are today. These are what the Bible speaks of as "death" in the widest sense. This is what Paul speaks of when he says "the wages of sin is death" (Romans 6:23)—not a corpse, but the sense of pain, sorrow, toil, and subjection.

It is true that engaging in sinful acts or thoughts yields a temporary pleasure. Indulgence in sin is ego-satisfying, but it is all a package deal. We cannot omit the bad parts and take only the good. It all goes together and contributes to the sense of loss familiar to all, a sense of emptiness within . . . the restlessness of our race.

In looking at God's word to Adam and Eve after the Fall, we must now more closely examine these factors of death to see what they involve and why they were given to the race. We greatly need to understand this, because to understand it properly is to change us from grumbling critics of life to grateful optimists, fulfilling that often-quoted definition of Christians: "completely fearless, continually cheerful, and constantly in trouble."

Let us listen to God speak:

> *To the woman he said, "I will greatly multiply your pain in childbearing; in pain you shall bring forth children, yet your desire shall be for your husband, and he shall rule over you"* (Genesis 3:16).

There is something very interesting here. God's approach to the woman is different than to the man, and certainly different than to the serpent. Notice that he says to the serpent, "Because you have done this . . ." and also to Adam, "Because you have listened . . ." But to the woman he makes no such charge of responsibility. There are consequences in her life that follow sin, but it is significant that he does not charge her with being ultimately at fault. We will see why when we come to God's word to Adam.

In each of these cases—the serpent's, the man's, and the woman's—there are two consequences that follow. We've already seen that the serpent was to experience continual humiliation and ultimate defeat. Now we learn that the consequences for the woman are pain and subjection. These factors arise out of her nature, and we must look more closely at them.

Bound to Her Children

First, there is the factor of *pain*. Undoubtedly this verse refers to the pain and danger of childbirth which women alone can experience. No man knows what a woman goes through in the birth of a child, but every mother understands. The word here refers to more than mere physical pain; it is basically the Hebrew word for *sorrow*. In Hebrew there is no word for pain, but sorrow is the word universally used. It comes from a root which means "to toil"; thus, heartbreaking toil. This is perhaps why there has come into our language a description of birth pains as "labor," toil of a heartbreaking variety. So this means more than simple physical pain; it refers also to the heartbreak associated with having children.

This heartbreak of rearing children is woman's primary experience as a result of the Fall. It means that a mother's sense of success or failure is related to her children. A threat to a child is pain to a mother's heart. Perhaps every mother feels more sharply than the father any sense of danger to or failure in her children. Mothers' hearts are bound to their children. We know this from experience and it is in line with what this passage suggests. The mother becomes so involved in the life of her children that what they feel, she feels; if they fail, she feels the heartbreak of it particularly strongly.

All this helps explain a very troublesome passage in the New Testament which has bothered many at times, found in Paul's first letter to Timothy:

> *I permit no woman to teach or to have authority over men; she is to keep silent. For Adam was formed first, then Eve; and Adam was not deceived, but the woman was deceived and became a*

transgressor. Yet woman will be saved through bearing children, if she continues in faith and love and holiness, with modesty (1 Timothy 2:12-15).

You can immediately see how difficult the passage is; no wonder many have struggled with exactly what it means. We will need to expand on a few things in its translation, but if we lay the amended passage alongside the passage in Genesis 3, things immediately become clearer.

First, when Paul speaks of the woman being "saved," it must be understood that he does not refer to her being regenerated, or born again. He is not talking about entrance into the Christian life. Women and men alike are saved in that sense on the same terms, by faith in Jesus Christ. In Christ "there is neither male nor female" (Galatians 3:28); all come on the same basis. What Paul is talking about here is how a woman finds fulfillment, the sense of satisfaction in life. You find this same use later in the letter, when the apostle says to Timothy:

Take heed to yourself and to your teaching; hold to that, for by so doing you will save both yourself and your hearers (1 Timothy 4:16).

Obviously he is not talking about redemption, in the sense of regeneration; he is talking about saving his life in terms of making it worthwhile, rendering it useful and purposeful. This is the sense in which it is used in the second chapter about women. Women will find their lives fulfilled through bearing children.

But the last phrase in 1 Timothy 2:15 begins not with "if she continues," but is literally in the Greek, "if *they* [that is, the children] continue in faith and love and holiness, with modesty." This accords exactly with what we find in Genesis, where it is suggested that a mother's heart is wrapped up with the life and career of her children. She lives in and by her children. The meaning of her life is revealed in them, and if they succeed, she has succeeded; but if they fail, she has failed. I think every mother will understand fully what I mean.

But there is more to woman's experience as a result of the Fall. We read further,

> . . . *yet your desire shall be for your husband,*
> *and he shall rule over you (Genesis 3:16).*

The phrase *your desire* is interesting. It comes from the Hebrew word for "leg" and means "to run after." She desires to run after her husband. This is not primarily a reference to passion, but to the hunger for approval. It is saying that a woman finds her fullest sense of satisfaction in gaining her husband's approval. No other can approach his approval in its significance to her. There can be no substitute for it. Others can be pleased and happy with her, but she doesn't care a fig. Her desire finds its fulfillment in her husband—she longs to be important to him.

Rivalry for Leadership

This desire is not in itself a consequence of sin. This relationship of woman to man was present before the Fall. The headship of the man was a fact from creation. It is the latter phrase of the sentence that marks the result of the Fall—"he shall rule over you." If we imagine ourselves back with Adam and Eve before the Fall in that blissful scene in the garden of Eden, we see that the relationship of the woman to the man consisted of a natural desire to follow. She came out of man and was made for him, to be his helper and to work toward his goals. It was a natural yielding to which she offered no resistance, but delighted in following the man.

But now, after the Fall, a perverse element enters. A struggle occurs, a tension ensues, in which the woman is torn between the natural God-given desire to yield to her husband, and the awakened desire to exert her will against his in a perverse urge to rivalry or domination. This is what creates tension in women as a result of the Fall. It means that in order to exert proper leadership, men must sometimes do so against the will of their wives. This constitutes "ruling" in the sense intended here. The struggle and tension produced in women's lives creates the tyranny that sometimes ensues in marriage, where the man rules with an iron hand. This is never justified in Scripture. Husbands are exhorted to love their wives and to deal patiently and kindly with them, as the Lord Jesus does the church. But in fallen man it results in the tyranny of man over woman, often as a result of the struggle within her.

Perhaps the most accurate description of this comes from a woman herself:

> *Millions of words have been written on how a man should love a woman. I would like to give you my reflections on the things a man should not do in loving a woman. First, don't yield your leadership. That's the main thing. Don't hand us the reins. We would consider this an abdication on your part. It would confuse us, it would alarm us, it would make us pull back.*

> *Quicker than anything else it would fog the clear vision that made us love you in the first place. Oh, we will try to get you to give up your position as number one in the house—that's the terrible con-*

*tradiction in us. We will seem to be fighting you
to the last inch for final authority on everything,
for awhile, but in the obscure recesses of our hearts
we want you to win. You have to win, for we
aren't really made for leadership. It's a pose.*

Would you like to know who wrote that? Judy Garland! It is the story of her own experiences with men (in *Coronet* magazine, February 1955).

This is why a woman can never find happiness in marriage until she takes seriously the words of Scripture: "Wives, be subject to your husbands, as to the Lord" (Ephesians 5:22).

One of the two major factors producing the terrible breakdown in marriage in our country today is the failure to understand this principle—that it is a woman's privilege, under God, to find fulfillment in submission to her husband's leadership. Wives are not to resist it, or try to rival him in these matters.

I am continually amazed at how much this needs to be asserted these days, especially among Christians. I heard recently of three Christian wives who raised this question in a discussion: If a woman believes the Lord wants her to do certain work at church or something else in connection with the Lord's work, and her husband doesn't want her to do it, what should she do? They decided that she should go ahead anyway, and if the husband objected or raised a fuss, it could be interpreted as suffering for Christ's sake.

I don't think I could find a more classic example of repeating the pattern of temptation found here in Genesis. There is the same subtle desire for an ego-satisfying activity, coupled with a rationalization that, in effect, cancels out God's word, thus permitting an activity that is contrary to what God wants.

It is God who said, "Wives be subject to your husbands as to the Lord." Therefore, he cannot be and is not pleased by wives who will not do so. No amount of justification will cancel out that disobedience, which usually results from a subtle form of desire for domination.

I would like to give another interesting quotation, this time from then Governor (now Senator) Mark Hatfield of Oregon who, in a very interesting article, tells how surprised reporters were when they discovered his wife had included the word "obey" in her marriage vows. He went on to discuss how he and his wife had come to the conviction that this word should be used:

> *I can recall the very evening that Antoinette first broached the subject. We had been invited to spend an evening at the home of married friends. Because we were considering marriage ourselves, perhaps we were sensitive to the relationship between this couple. At any rate, something about them puzzled us.*

> *Then, driving home, we suddenly put our finger on it. The wife, and not the husband, had taken charge of the evening. "Charles, dear," she had said as we came through the door, "won't you take their coats to the bedroom?" And later, "The phone is ringing, Charles." And still later, "Charles, don't you think it's time for some refreshments?" And each time Charles jumped up from his chair and dutifully did her bidding.*

> *Oddly, Charles is not a Mr. Milquetoast; he is an aggressive businessman with a reputation as a go-getter. Nor is his wife mannish or overtly bossy. They are normal, average, likable people.*

In fact, I think it was the normalcy of the situation that alarmed us. The wife was the head of that household and nobody, least of all Charles, saw anything wrong in it.

As I drove home that night, Antoinette suddenly said, "When I get married, I want a husband, not a partner." I looked at her in surprise. "What do you mean?" "Perhaps I mean that I don't think there can be a real partnership in marriage," she replied. "It's like this car. We're traveling along together going to the same place, but you're driving. Both of us can't drive. And I don't think there can be two drivers in a marriage, either. One person's got to be at the wheel, and when it's the woman, I don't like what it does to her. Or to him. But it hurts her most."

Those are wise words, reflecting exactly the position of Scripture in this matter.

But I'm sure some women are thinking, "What a raw deal we've been handed. Talk about cruel and unusual punishment, this is it." But is it? Is this intended to be punishment? These words are often interpreted as though all this is a punishment dealt out by God upon the race, and woman's lot is the heaviest of all. But it is not punishment and was never intended to be punishment. As we look together at God's word to Adam, you will see why.

And to Adam he said, "Because you have listened to the voice of your wife, and have eaten of the tree of which I commanded you, 'You shall not eat of it,' cursed is the ground because of you; in toil you shall eat of it all the days of your life; thorns and thistles it shall bring forth to you; and you shall eat the plants of the field. In the sweat of your

face you shall eat bread till you return to the
ground, for out of it you were taken; you are dust,
and to dust you shall return" (Genesis 3:17-19).

In these verses we learn for the first time the nature
of the sin that caused the Fall. It was not merely that
Adam ate the fruit in disobedience to God. There was
something before that, and God records it. "Because
you have listened to the voice of your wife." This was
the sin that began the fall of Adam and brought the
misery of death upon the human race.

Now there are times when the wisest thing a man
can do is to listen to the voice of his wife. Many a
woman gives excellent advice to her husband, and a
man is foolish who does not pay attention to what his
wife says. Surely Pontius Pilate would have saved
himself grief if he had listened when his wife sent him
word concerning Jesus, "Have nothing to do with
that righteous man, for I have suffered much over
him today in a dream" (Matthew 27:19). But he ig-
nored his wife's voice, which would have saved him.

Whatever You Say, Dear

But here Adam is charged with guilt because he
listened to his wife's voice—*when it was different from
the voice of God!* That is the point. It was wrong for
him to take his leadership from her. It was a denial of
the headship God had established. Paul gives us the
order of headship when he says, "The head of every
man is Christ, the head of a woman is her husband,
and the head of Christ is God" (1 Corinthians 11:3).
It was also the apostle Paul who tells us that Adam
was not deceived in the Fall. The woman was deceived. She was deluded, for she believed the enemy.
She thought he meant it when he said they would become like God if they ate the fruit.

But Adam was not fooled. He knew if they ate the fruit the Fall would follow—that they would lose their relationship to God, and that they would die. He knew it, but he deliberately disobeyed God and set his wife above God. He denied the headship of Christ over himself and surrendered his own headship over the woman.

This has been man's major failure in marriage ever since, and the second major cause producing chaos in marriage today: a man who refuses to lead, a man who turns over to his wife the ultimate responsibility of the family. He views his sphere as that of making a living and gives to her the job of making a life. He refuses to make decisions, refuses to give direction or to show concern over the way the family is going, refuses to enter into the problems of child discipline and training. All this constitutes failure and the breakdown of man's headship over woman and of God's headship over man.

This highlights two basic false concepts in marriage for us. One is that a man, when he gets married, is to please his wife by doing whatever she wants to do. Usually this results in the chinless, spineless, supine Caspar Milquetoast kind of individual. But it is a widespread approach to marriage today, and sociologists tell us it is rapidly producing in our country a matriarchal society. When boys, reared at home, do not have a male image to relate to, they do not know what a father is supposed to be—they never see one—so they relate to their mother and the mother becomes the dominant factor in the family. This turns society upside-down and produces much of the weakness, conflict, and violence we see so widely today.

The second false concept in marriage is that the husband, regarding himself as the head, may do whatever he wants—that he is to run the home to suit himself, and his pleasure determines what occurs. He becomes a tyrant, a dictator. This is as wrong as the first view, and is equally contrary to the Word of God.

The truth is that he, too, is under authority. He is to submit to the headship of Jesus Christ. He is to follow him. If a man refuses to do that, his home is bound to go on the rocks one way or another, either in internal conflict or in actual outward breakup. He is to follow the Lord Jesus Christ, who reveals himself in God's word and in prayer. A husband is to follow Christ whether he and his wife feel like it or not—that's the whole issue. He is kindly but firmly to insist that *they* are to do what God wants.

Toil and Death

Because Adam refused to do that and listened rather to his wife, letting her determine the course of the marriage, the Fall resulted. Two things came from it. First: *toil.* The ground was cursed, and thorns and thistles appeared and covered the ground. This suggests an immediate lowering of fertility. Nature produces only in response to God's continuing bestowal of power. All God needs to do to change the course of nature is to reduce that flow of power, and lower fertility results. Nature then goes out of balance; the result is an increase in strong plants, such as thorns and thistles. This reflects the eccentricity which has come to mankind. Nature is out of balance because man is out of balance.

This is why we must struggle so to make a living. Man is reduced to unending toil and sorrow. It is interesting that the word *toil* is exactly the same word in Hebrew that is translated *pain* for the woman. It is heartbreaking sorrow, caused by labor and toil. This is the reason for the "rat race" of life, why we are constantly under pressure to get more out of a reluctant nature.

Work is not the curse given to man; work is a blessing. It is toil that is the curse. If you do not have work to do, you are of all people most miserable. Work is a blessing from God; but hard, grinding, toiling work is the result of the Fall.

The second factor resulting from Adam's failure to observe his headship is *death*. God said, "In the sweat of your face you shall eat bread till you return to the ground, for out of it you were taken; you are dust, and to dust you shall return." This sense of death lurking at life's boundaries gives us a feeling of futility about life.

Remember what God said to the rich man who built barns, filled them up, and then said to himself, "Soul, take your ease, for you have all you need." God said to him that night, "Fool! This night your soul is required of you." And God asked this question: "The things you have prepared, whose will they be?" (Luke 12:16-21). Yes, that is the question death forces us to face. You struggle to amass property, all the good things of life. But what a sense of futility there is in having to pass them along to somebody else, someone who didn't turn a finger to gain them.

Years ago a young friend of mine mentioned to an older man, "My uncle died a millionaire."

"He did not," the man replied.

"What do you mean?" my young friend said. "You didn't know my uncle. How do you know he didn't die a millionaire?"

The older man said simply, "Who has the million now?"

No, no one dies a millionaire. Naked we came into the world and naked we will leave it. We have

nothing we can take with us; we must leave it all behind. We are dust, and to dust we will return.

Is It Punishment?

There is the sentence of God—pain, subjection,
toil, and death. Is this punishment? I promised to
face this question with you. Is it punishment? Is this
the result of our folly, for which we must grind our
teeth and struggle all our life? Is it our curse for what
Adam did?

No, it is not. It appears to be punishment only
when we refuse it and resist it or rebel against it. But
these things were never intended to be any kind of
punishment.

They are instead intended to help us, to be means
by which we are reminded of truth. Their purpose is
to counteract the subtle pride which the enemy has
planted in our race and which keeps us imagining all
kinds of illusory things, these arrogant pretensions
we constantly make—that we can solve all our problems, that we are the captain of our fate and the mas-
ter of our soul.

But we are constantly reminded that these things
are not true. Death, pain, toil and subjection are
limits we cannot escape. They cancel out our egocen-
tric dreams and reduce us to seeing ourselves as we
really are: We are dust. We are but men. We are limited, dependent. We cannot go it alone—we desperately need other people, and we desperately need
God. The hour of our greatest hope is when our eyes
are opened to this fact and we say, "Lord, I can't make
it without you. I need you desperately."

Who of us has not seen a loved one suddenly pass
away, and in the presence of death we sensed that we
were facing a stark fact which could not be explained
away or covered up or shoved under the rug? There it

was, facing us every time we turned around. It was to remind us of what we are, and where we are. You will find this principle running all through the Bible. Jacob limped on his leg for the rest of his life after wrestling with the angel at the brook of Peniel. It was to remind him that he was a man, nothing but a man, dependent on God. It was to turn him from reliance on his own craftiness and the cleverness of his own wit. Moses was denied the right to enter into the land because of his failure. It was a reminder to him, who had been given great prestige and power before God, that he was nothing but a man and that he could live only within the limitations set by God.

A sword came upon David's house because of his sin. It was a constant reminder to him that though he was king he could not do his own will or act as he pleased. He was a man, dependent on God. Paul had a thorn in the flesh given to him, and he cried out against it. But God reminded him that it was given to keep him humble, that he might be a useful instrument in God's hands, dependent on his love and grace.

Remember the closing words of Psalms 23?

> *Surely goodness and mercy shall follow me all the days of my life; and I shall dwell in the house of the LORD for ever.*

One quaint commentator has said those words *goodness* and *mercy* are God's sheepdogs. David wrote this "Shepherd's Psalm" when he was but a lad keeping sheep, and we can picture God's goodness and mercy to be like sheepdogs that nip at the heels of the flock and keep them in line, driving them into place. In the same way, surely God's goodness and mercy shall follow me all the days of my life, nipping at my heels, humiliating me, turning me back from whatever looks good but is really evil, keeping me from getting what I wrongly think I need and want. In the end we must name these guardians what God names them—goodness and mercy!

No, these things are not punishment. They are the disciplines of grace. They are what Paul refers to in Hebrews 12. If you are not chastised, disciplined by God, you are not a child of his. These things are given to bring you into subjection, for God loves you, and he wants you to be what he made you to be—and what your own heart longs to attain. Your pride needs to be crushed and humiliated, your ego smashed, your dependence on yourself broken. Your reliance on your abilities, your background, and your education needs to be pulled out from under you—until you lean upon the God who made you and who is able to supply all that you need.

And as you do this, you will discover that "whoever would save his life will lose it, and whoever loses his life for my sake will find it" (Matthew 16:25).

10
EXIT FROM EDEN

To understand this last scene, let us review quickly what we have learned so far. We have looked at the process of temptation—the arousing of desire, the mind's rationalization of that desire, and thus the moving of the will to an act of disobedience. This is the process temptation follows, always and forever.

Then we saw how death immediately entered the scene. What the Bible means by death is far more than simply the ending of life. In the sense this account reveals, death is first a vivid feeling of self-consciousness. We are made immediately aware of ourselves, and this brings with it shame, guilt, and fear. There is also a sense of defensiveness, a desire to blame somebody else; and then a great sense of loss or limitation, an enslavement. These were inevitable after Adam's sin, just as they are for us.

The next step is repentance. We have seen how God, in grace, skill, and tenderness, leads this guilty pair back along the path they have come, and helps them see what they have done. Repentance consists of two things. First, the awareness of the course of temptation: It comes from within. God helps Adam see that his sin arose not from anything outside of him but from something within. Second, the pair acknowledge the fact of their disobedience. They both come to the place where they say, "Yes, we ate."

Following their confession, God gives a promise of grace. He announces defeat for the tempter and declares his judgment. Then he provides certain helps to the man and woman to keep them clinging in dependence on God, which is the only place of safety, the only place of security and strength in life. These helps are pain, subjection, toil, and death.

Changed for Life

This brings us to the last three steps of the process traced in this chapter, and these three are extremely significant. After God acts in grace to give a great promise, and sets "sheepdogs" nipping at the heels of mankind to bring men and women into the place of blessing—what happens next? The first thing is an act of faith on Adam's part:

> *The man called his wife's name Eve, because she*
> *was the mother of all living (Genesis 3:20).*

In order to understand this we must link it immediately with verse 15 where we have God's statement to the serpent about the woman:

*I will put enmity between you and the woman,
and between your seed and her seed; he shall
bruise your head, and you shall bruise his heel.*

This verse deals with the woman's progeny, the
seed of the woman. Verse 20 deals with the same. The
woman is to become "the mother of all living." In response to this promise of a seed to come through the
woman, Adam changes his wife's name. In the beginning, her name was not Eve, but Adam called her
Ishsha which is the Hebrew for woman:

*Then the man said, "This at last is bone of my
bones and flesh of my flesh; she shall be called
Woman [Ishsha], because she was taken out of
Man [Ish] (Genesis 2:23).*

He called her "Out of Man," and that was her original name. But now, because of God's promise, he
changes her name to *Chavah,* which means "Life."
Our English word *Eve* is simply an anglicization of
this Hebrew word *Chavah.*

Ordinarily verse 20 is taken to indicate Adam's understanding that a race of men and women are to
come from Eve; thus, she is to be the mother of all
living. But that was rather obvious from the beginning. Adam and Eve knew they were to be mother
and father of a race, because God told them to multi-
ply and fill the earth. But this verse, you will notice,
immediately follows the announcement of man's ultimate doom, death. God said to Adam, "You are dust,
and to dust you shall return." Adam understands that
he is to become the father of a doomed race; that because of his sin, his descendants are doomed to death
from the moment of birth.

How certainly we know the truth of this! We begin
to die the moment we are born, and the process goes

on until it results in the inevitable conclusion of the grave. I am always faintly amused by the optimistic reports of the medical profession about the present increase of life span, though I am sure this is progress and is something good. But there is always the implication that ultimately we are going to win this battle. We have indeed won great victories in the medical field; yet the death rate has remained exactly as always—a flat one hundred percent.

Adam realizes this is true. But if you read carefully here you will notice something important: Adam changes his wife's name because Eve has heard God's promise and believed it. This is the only possible explanation for verse 20. When a human being, guilty in sin, believes the promise of God, he or she passes immediately from death into life. In recognition of that change, Adam calls his wife *Life,* because she has passed from death into life.

"Therefore," he says, "she is the mother of all living," that is, the first of a long line of those who would pass from death into life. This ties in exactly with the promise of the seed of the woman which would ultimately come and which would bruise the serpent's head. All those associated with Christ become part of this redeemed humanity, which is the seed of the woman, and Eve was the first of that line.

All this corresponds with the significance attached throughout the Bible to a change of name. Have you noticed how many biblical characters change their names, and always with this same significance? It means a person has also changed his nature, his character. He has become a different person.

A bit later in Genesis we learn that God changed the name of Abram to Abraham, and the name of his wife from Sarai to Sarah. These new names were significant. Later he changed the name of Jacob (which means "a supplanter, a usurper") to Israel (which means "prince with God"). It is always *God* who changes these names. In the New Testament our Lord changed Simon's name to Peter (meaning "rock"), for Peter would become like a rock in the early church. Saul of Tarsus becomes Paul, which means "little"— Paul had lost his conceit and become little in his own eyes.

This new name for the woman therefore reflects not a promise that Eve was to be the mother of all human beings, but rather that she is to be the mother of all those who would find life through Jesus Christ. The immediate response to the promise of God is an act of faith on Adam's part. After all, this is the only proper response to a promise; to believe it and to act on it. And that is what Adam did.

Throughout this chapter there are only two things man can and does do with regard to the problem of sin: repent and believe. That is all. He exercises repentance and faith. Throughout the rest of the Bible, repentance and faith are the means by which the problem of human evil is handled—repentance as an acknowledgment of the facts, and faith as a laying hold of God's promise by an act of the will. It is thus that man lays hold of God's grace.

Mark of Acceptance

Now the divine activity begins again:

> *And the LORD God made for Adam and for his wife garments of skins, and clothed them (Genesis 3:21).*

We have already noted the significance of this in part. This was a sign of God's redemptive activity. With the sacrifice of another life he clothed Adam and Eve. It is a beautiful picture of how we are clothed with the righteousness of Christ. We are given his standing before the Father.

But clothing is not required for God's benefit. It does not make any difference to God that Adam and Eve are naked. In fact, as Hebrews 4:13 tells us, we are all always naked before God: Everything is naked and open in his sight. It is not God who requires this clothing, nor is it Adam and Eve, though it may have bothered them to be naked before God in their fallen condition. But it is because of the others who would see them that they are clothed. Clothing is for *public* appearance. God desires the mark of his acceptance and the acknowledgment of it to be plain to the whole universe. This is why Adam and Eve are clothed, and it is the primary purpose of clothing.

We are concerned about clothing today because it makes us acceptable in the eyes of others. We think we look better with clothing, and most others think so too. In the New Testament story of the prodigal son, the first thing the father did when the son returned home was to clothe him with a new robe. It is a public mark of acceptance, a public demonstration that he was back in full favor with his father. In the story of the healing of the demoniac of Gadara, we are told that the Lord cast a legion of demons out of this man, and when local townspeople came to the scene, they found the former demoniac sitting at the feet of Jesus, "clothed and in his right mind" (Mark 5:15). His clothing was a significant expression of his return to normalcy.

The importance of clothing was underscored for me one day as I drove down the street near where youngsters were getting out of high school. I passed by three boys, all clothed rather shabbily. Two of them were not so bad, but one of them was in a terrible state. His clothes were filthy, his hair was matted and dirty, and I found him revolting to look at.

But it set me thinking. What makes these young-sters dress this way? Why are they so fiercely deter-mined about it? Why is it so important to them to dress in this fashion in defiance of authorities and cus-toms and traditions? As I thought it over, I recalled this story of Adam being clothed by God. I saw im-mediately that what lies behind the fierce desire of young people to dress in these weird fashions is that clothing reflects the inner condition of the heart. We want our clothing to express what we are. The young people's dress is therefore an attempt, in some sense, to be honest.

When I thought of it that way I could see that perhaps we are superficial in our attempts to correct these conditions by outward legislation. If clothing does reflect an inner condition, it does not help much to force an outward change. Clothing means some-thing. The proof is that whenever any of these young people (as I have seen happen several times now) be-come converted and their inner rebellion ceases, the first sign is that their clothing and hairstyle change. Their whole outward look changes because the in-ward attitude has changed.

Notice that it was *God* who clothed Adam and Eve. He killed the animals, made the skins, and clothed them. They did not even clothe themselves, but he dressed them. It is important that we let God do this to us. Not long ago a young man came to me bur-dened by a moral failure in his life. He was heavy with guilt and he talked it all out with me. Together we went through the Scriptures, but he said to me, "Yes, I know these things. I know God has forgiven me, but I can't forgive myself. I feel unclean, and I can't look at myself as being anything but unclean."

Then I retold the story of Peter on the housetop in

Joppa, when he was waiting for an unknown delega-
tion to come for Cornelius. God prepared him for that
encounter by letting down a sheet from heaven, filled
with unclean and clean animals, and said to him,
"Rise, Peter, kill and eat." Peter protested and said,
"No, Lord, I have never touched anything unclean in
my life." God immediately rebuked him, "Peter,
don't you call unclean what I have called clean" (see
Acts 10:9-15).

I said to this young man, "Isn't this what God is
saying to you? The Scripture says, 'If we confess our
sins, he is faithful and just, and will forgive our sins
and cleanse us from all unrighteousness' (1 John
1:9). Now don't you dare to call unclean what God
has cleansed. That's an insult to God's grace." He immediately saw the point and was tremendously
helped.

Thus, following Adam's act of faith, God cleanses
him and publicly marks his acceptance so that it is
clear throughout the universe that Adam and Eve are
received of God and owned again by him.

If this is the case, then how shall we explain this
last section which seems to be totally inconsistent?

> *Then the LORD God said, "Behold, the man has
> become like one of us, knowing good and evil; and
> now, lest he put forth his hand and take also of
> the tree of life, and eat, and live for ever"—there-
> fore the LORD God sent him forth from the gar-
> den of Eden, to till the ground from which he was
> taken. He drove out the man; and at the east of
> the garden of Eden he placed the cherubim, and a
> flaming sword which turned every way, to guard
> the way to the tree of life (Genesis 3:22-24).*

God seems to have drastically changed his attitude, hasn't he? He had just accepted Adam and

Eve and dressed them in new clothing that he himself had provided; but now suddenly he banishes them from his presence, drives them out, slams and locks the door behind them, and sets a guard in the path to keep them from coming back in. Isn't something wrong here?

The Way to the Tree

If we read this passage that way, we have surely misread it. Note carefully exactly what it says. Notice that verse 22 is one of the few unfinished sentences in the Bible. God acknowledges that man has fallen into a condition of self-centeredness. He says, "The man has now become like one of us." Man knows good and evil by relating it to himself. This is the basic problem with mankind. We have no right to know good and evil by relating it to ourselves, but that is what we do all the time.

It is recorded in Judges 17:6, "Every man did what was right in his own eyes." That is the formula for anarchy. It means we judge everything by the way it appears to us. This is the way God does it, for he is the measure of all things; but it is wrong for man to judge this way. God acknowledges this condition, and having done so, he now faces the problem of the other tree in the garden.

This is not the tree of the knowledge of good and evil, but the tree of life. God says, "What if man, doomed now to guilt, shame, limitation, and loss, should reach forth his hand and take and eat of the tree of life, and live forever?" It would mean that man would never physically die but would go on in his evil condition forever. Notice that God leaves the sentence hanging in the air as though the result is too terrible to describe. What if man should do this?

God's loving solution follows. He says, "Drive

him out, cast him out of the garden, and put at the gate of Eden the cherubim" (from elsewhere in Scripture we learn that cherubim are what we might call angelic animals, related to the holiness of God), and a flaming sword which turns every way—and notice this—"to guard the way *to* the tree of life." It does not say, "to keep men from coming to the tree of life." This is not what the barrier is for. It is to guard the way *to* the tree of life, so that men come to it the right way and not the wrong way.

So, although this passage is usually read as though God has barred man from the tree of life, and there is no way to get back in, that is not true. There is a way in, but it is no longer a physical way. This is what this text tells us. Man must be kept from trying to come to it through some physical means, but must be forced to find the right way back. This is what the cherubim and the flaming sword are for. They absolutely cut off any other way to God than the right way. There is only one way—and no other.

This is why what you do in the way of religion with your body is of no importance whatever unless it is a genuine reflection of what you do with your spirit. This explains why you can come to church every Sunday morning, sit in the pews, bow your head, pray, stand, sit down again, genuflect—anything you want; but if the heart is not doing the same thing it is an ugly, distasteful thing in God's sight, and he has no regard for it at all. There is no way to come to God by *doing* something; none at all. The physical approach to God is completely cut off.

The Tree Is for Healing

But now read the words of the Lord Jesus in John 14:6.

*I am the way, and the truth, and the life; no one
comes to the Father, but by me.*

This is the only way there is. It is the way to begin
the Christian life, but it is also the way to continue
the Christian life. Do you know the way to the tree of
life? In Revelation 22:2 we read that the tree of life is
for healing. Do you know how to find healing? When
your spirit has been torn and broken, when you are
pressed by despair, or wounded by sorrow or grief or
heartache or guilt, whatever it may be, do you know
the way to the place of healing, to the place where the
living waters flow? Have you learned to go not just
once, but many, many times; to drink again and
again of the water of life? Do you know what this
means?

Do you know what Jesus meant when he said to
the woman at the well, "I will put in you a well of
living water, so that you do not need to come to this
well for satisfaction. You will find it within you, and
you can drink any time you want to" (John 4:14)?
Have you learned to drink of this well within when
the pressure is on; to retreat from outward circumstances for the moment and come again to that
living fountain of water, springing up within you? To
take by quiet faith his promised supply, to partake of
his patience and his power, and so meet circumstances with a mind at ease, relaxed, trusting, no
longer fearful? Do you know what this means? This is
the function of the tree of life.

This physical exclusion from Eden is why man's
body must die. The apostle Paul tells us that this is so
even for Christians: "We know that our old self was
crucified with him *so that the sinful body might be de-
stroyed*" (Romans 6:6)—that we might live with

Christ in the realm of the spirit and soul. This is why our bodies are dying and we cannot come to God physically. We cannot find our way visibly into his presence until the problem of the body is resolved in resurrection. But the glorious truth is, as Hebrews 10:19-20 declares to us, that the blood of Jesus Christ has opened for us a new and living way into the holy place, and there again we live in the presence of the tree of life in the garden of Eden. Spiritually and psychologically (in the realm of emotions and thoughts) we are to live in the presence of God because a way has been opened back to the tree of life.

Let me summarize the teaching of this passage. Look at the whole process.

First, *temptation*. How familiar we are with that!

It is followed immediately by *death*, which grips us and casts a gloom over our lives, bores us and frustrates us, and makes us despairing, discouraged, and defeated.

Then we come to the place of *repentance*, where we admit the facts as God sees them.

Then we experience the flowing of *grace*, the promise of victory and restoration, accompanied by those helpful measures through which we are made to see our dependence upon him.

Next, our spirit responds and in *faith* we believe what God has said and are changed and strengthened. We are remade by what the New Testament calls "the renewing of the mind by the Holy Spirit."

Then there is public *acknowledgment* on God's part, as he clothes us with Christ's peace, Christ's righteousness, Christ's power and poise, so that we become panic-proof, no longer disturbed by circumstances.

The process ends as we find our way back to the

healing of our mind, heart, and spirit—spiritual health!

Isn't this also what the New Testament develops for us? Can you see how clearly these opening chapters in Genesis are from the hand and mind of God? The whole gospel of grace is given to us right at the beginning, so we might live in this world, amid all life's problems.

The way back is open to all of us, the way to the One who himself is the tree of life—the way, the truth, and the life.

We have no other place to live in these days. Each of us, young and old alike, must grasp more firmly the vast importance of learning to live by the Lord Jesus, by a constant communication with his life, his grace, his strength, his power. Let us open our eyes to understand these things and live by them, so that those around will be mystified to know where we get this amazing strength, this unflappable poise, this startling and unfailing ability to handle life at its worst.

We can do it through the power of Almighty God.

And we must.